Ultimate Questions

A Theological Primer

Ultimate Questions

A Theological Primer

Clyde F. Crews

Paulist Press
New York/Mahwah

The Publisher gratefully acknowledges the use of the following: "Widow McFarlane" and "Lucinda Matlock" by Edgar Lee Masters from the *Spoon River Anthology*, published by Macmillan & Co. and reprinted by permission of Ellen C. Masters; excerpts from p. 100 of *Our Town* by Thornton Wilder, copyright 1938, 1957 by Thornton Wilder, reprinted by special permission of Harper & Row, Publishers, Inc.; excerpts from English translation of *The Roman Missal* © 1973, International Committee on English in the Liturgy, Inc. All rights reserved. Used by permission.

Library of Congress
Catalog Card Number: 85–62935

ISBN: 0–8091–2774–1

Published by Paulist Press
997 Macarthur Boulevard
Mahwah, N.J. 07430

Printed and bound in the United States of America

Contents

Introduction

The Baffle of Being

We all carry mysteries around inside of us. That is part of both the freight and fragility of being human. From a certain point of view, our very lives are questions or sets of questions put to us about who we are and what we shall be. No one escapes the questioning; and in good measure we are defined in life and even in death by the nature of our own personal response.

Some people hide from the fundamental questions and spend their lives in a frenzy of evasions, busy projects, higher and higher standards of physical or material success. A day or even an evening spent in the quietness of their own company makes them edgy if not downright frightened. Others rush headlong into the ultimate things and become obsessed with them, diminishing their ability to appreciate the here, the now, the ordinary.

And whenever the basic life questions have to be faced, people invariably have a mixed collection of reactions. Some experience fear; some bitterness or skepticism; others find new levels of hope, of compassion, of commitment to the human endeavor. It is the thought of Anglo-American poet W.H. Auden (1907–1973) who describes to some extent the position with which this study approaches the questioning. "The funniest of mortals, and the kindest," Auden wrote, "are those who are most aware of the baffle of being."

It is one thing to maintain that all individuals should at some point or points face primal things articulately in their lives; it is something else again for an academic institution to make such a consideration a fundamental part of its own academic concerns, even requirements. By what right does an institution of objective higher learning make such a requirement? Or, put another way, how is it possible for a liberal arts college to respect religious diversity, wide toleration and dissent, and yet provide a searching and respectful study of classical human and religious values?

This last question was the challenge put to a group of twenty specially invited teams from private colleges and universities across the United States at a conference sponsored by the Danforth Foundation in 1975. It was out of that question and challenge that Bellarmine College in Louisville, one of the Danforth participants, formulated both a revised charter of purpose and an Ultimate Questions course for all undergraduate arts and sciences majors.

In a section of the Bellarmine Charter of Purpose titled "Ultimate Questions" is to be found a rationale for both the college's concern and for the course requirement:

> This college calls upon all members of the academic community to address themselves to ultimate questions about reality and human life: the meaning of God, freedom, society, suffering and death, care and hope. It is when men and women have come to grips with questions such as these, and have achieved some measure of carefully considered response, that they begin to advance toward educated maturity.

The desired result, then, is not a "party line" collection of simple answers to complex questions; nor, on the other hand, is it "epistemological silliness," the notion that in the vast cafeteria of ideas one is absolutely as good as another, equally treasured in the western tradition.

Rather, the goal is the serious pursuit of the questions as evidenced in western philosophy, religion, literature, the arts and sciences, along with "some measure of carefully considered response." The ultimate answers, as far as the students are concerned, are not and cannot be merely handed over by faculty, digested by students, and barked back on examinations. Students are asked to become aware of major responses of the western world and then to search their own minds and experiences for personal approaches to the primal puzzles. So, no theological or philosophic position is ever imposed or demanded either subtly or overtly. But a thorough knowledge of options and a coming to grips with them and their implications are very much expected in this kind of pursuit.

All of this presupposes a wider liberal arts context, of course—a familiarity with many academic fields, from economics to philosophy, from biology to commerce. Whatever works to add a significant piece to the human puzzle becomes appropriate.

And what are the appropriate attitudes with which to approach so profound a study? A respect for evidence, honesty, openness; a fundamental orientation toward conscience, responsible freedom, self-discovery, and continuing self-development. It may be noted here that such attitudes will not only be salutary to individuals who practice them; they also must inevitably have a social impact as students learn to think more clearly, experience the human situation more deeply and widely, and act more justly. In short, a tour of duty on the ultimate questions front leads not just to a reverence for the past, but also to an increased awareness of our own fragilities. And such a study may mean a critical evaluation of things as they are in the light of what they might be.

This study approaches the ultimate human questions under four major units or headings:

I. **Diverse Expressions of the Ultimate Questions**
A listing of several such questions as classically expressed, and an examination of their appearance in all human lives and all academic disciplines.

II. **Thoughtful Responses**
The growth of secularity in the nineteenth and twentieth centuries. An examination of several attempts to respond to the

ultimate things without reference to religious categories or expression.

III. The Religious Response
A study of fundamental definitions and critiques of religion; of elements common to all the world religions and of distinctive features of the major spiritualities of the east and west.

IV. The Christian Response
Major themes of the main-line Christian responses to ultimate questions.

Unit One:

Diverse Expressions

1

Soundings

"We don't know one millionth of one percent about anything." Thomas Edison (1847–1931)

This unit of study has three basic points to make:

(1) Persistence. The ultimate questions are not just an academic exercise. They are a keenly experienced, unavoidable part of any mature life.

(2) Dimensionality. Human life is not to be understood on its surface, or by its facts alone; it is also a matter of interpretations and meanings. There exists along with our "ordinary" level of living a difficult-to-define depth or mystery dimension to the human experience.

(3) Pervasiveness. The ultimate questions or mysteries make themselves known not only in personal experiences and lives; they also pervade every field of academic study, the arts, sciences, professions. Ultimate questions do not belong just to philosophers or "religious fanatics." They are intensely human puzzlements.

Walk into any major department or discount store in America and you walk at the same time into a world of warranties, guarantees, instructions, consumer information. From laundering instructions to installation hints, it is a world of precision, of credit card certitudes.

By striking contrast, when a child comes forth from the womb, there are no guarantees, no instructions taped to the wrists. It is highly likely that many people would welcome the cozy security of having a script provided for them to follow from their birth. But reality is not so obliging. In a wider sense, as we will later argue, insecurity and uncertainty can be claimed as one of the great benefits of the human enterprise. But, for now, let it be said that we are born with certain sets of *facts:* the regulation number of arms, lungs and brain cells. But what these facts are *for,* what they signify, that is in the realm of *interpretation.* And interpretations are a matter of human discovery and creation.

As a result, humanity has often enough been described as the questioning animal. It is part of our most deep-seated drives to want *to know.* We desire to know not only for practical reasons, but often for the sheer kick of the knowing experience. "All men by nature," Aristotle (384–322) solemnly assures his readers on the first page of his *Metaphysics,* "desire to know." (They may not desire to *learn;* that is a different matter.) If you don't believe Aristotle, believe the daytime soaps or the late-night gangster films: any character worth the salt wants to know the awful truth no matter how grisly it might be. They want to *know* about being embezzled or betrayed or two-timed, even if it takes the marrow out of their lives.

The individual and the race cannot stop questioning. Even if an individual ends by taking his or her own life, the invariable first response of coroner as well as family and friends is—why? On a less dramatic level, it would probably startle each of us to discover just how many questions we pose in the course of a single day.

The very fact of such persistent questioning tells us something about ourselves and also provides certain clues about the way reality itself might be structured.

Some questions are simply more vital, more profound, more foundational than others. To ask the time of day, the price of ginger ale, the distance from Omaha to Little Rock—these, as a general rule, would be simple questions without a great deal of emotional weight attached. Ask, however, if you can trust your best friend, if you have a lethal infection or not, if a profession is right or wrong for you . . . and the stakes go up decidedly. A question is ultimate when it concerns the very foundation of my life and meaning. From its Latin roots, the word ultimate suggests that which is situated beyond the immediate or the obvious; that which carries final weight; that which we might today refer to as "bottom line." But rather than spend more energies in definitions, we will shortly attempt a sample listing of some of the more classical formulations of ultimate questions.

But this much might be useful to say at the outset. Ultimate questions have a way of lurking beneath the most ordinary appearances. That is precisely why liberal arts education concerns itself with their study. Even the most casual discussion or argument or questions can be quickly enough pushed back to more primal considerations.

Raise a question about dating manners or about nuclear weapons; about salary levels or about abortion; about one-way streets or about civil rights. Before long it becomes apparent that either very critical philosophic questions or basic assumptions are at work underneath. If these do not surface or flare, it is usually because the parties to the discussion are making similar value assumptions in the first place.

What, then, are some of the ultimate questions that would be easily familiar to all the great thinkers of both east and west? The following listing is a modest attempt at a first skirmish with the primal inquiries.

1. *The Question of Purpose*
   - Why is there anything at all rather than nothing?
   - What is my own purpose in being on the earth?
   - On the cosmic level it can be asked if there is a destiny for higher life forms in the universe . . . or is all that we know nothing more than a cosmic accident without purpose whatsoever?
   - On the more personal level, there is the puzzle as to what I am making of my own individual life. Am I pursuing the right career? Am I making of my life all that it can be?

2. *The Question of Meaning*
   - Why do we keep asking *why*? There is a great mystery resident in this three letter word.
   - Why are facts alone never quite enough for us, so that we constantly seek out meanings, patterns, significance, in both the great and the minor events of life?
   - And why isn't the meaning of things *clear* . . . agreeable and available to all?

3. *The Question of Divinity*
   - Is humanity alone in the universe?
   - Are there other intelligences on other planets?
   - And more significantly, is there an Intelligence or Source that is at the ground of it all?
   - Have we been created by a benevolent reality that continues to care actively for each of us?
   - Are there evidences of the existence of such a provident being?
   - Is belief in God realism or is it escapism?

4. *The Question of Pain*
   - Why do we find such a load of conflict, contradiction, frustration and suffering within ourselves and around ourselves?
   - Does suffering too have a point or is it cruel and pointless?
   - Why, in particular, do ''the innocent'' suffer?

- Why must all things that live ultimately die?
- Is death itself a finality?

5. *The Question of Hope*
   - Why are resiliency, hope and rebirth such constant factors in the human experience?
   - What accounts for the amazing drive for life and meaning even when humanity finds itself in the most desperate situations?
   - What is the source and meaning of this "life force" or rage to live that such modern writers as Freud and Fromm have documented for humanity as a whole?

6. *The Question of Character*
   - What are the qualities or characteristics that I most admire in others and want others to find in me?
   - Why have essentially all peoples and cultures preferred, honored, and encouraged certain character qualities while dishonoring others? For example:

courage	over	cowardice
honesty		falseness
compassion		egotism
humor		glumness
justice		injustice
freedom		oppression
harmony		turmoil
beauty		ugliness
patience		rudeness
fidelity		promiscuity

7. *The Question of Resources*
   - What are my own particular strengths and weaknesses?
   - What special talents do I have and do I use them effectively?

- What are the resources of the community and nation of which I am a part? How effectively are they used? shared?

8. *The Question of Morality*
   - Where do we find the source of our experience of right and wrong?
   - Is our conviction of right and wrong, as C.S. Lewis says, a clue to the meaning of the universe?
   - Do right and wrong have an objective basis? To what extent can they be codified and specified either in religious morality or in law?
   - How much freedom do we truly have to make significant choices in our lives?

Further Reading

Adler, Mortimer. *Six Great Ideas* (New York: 1981).

Carmody, Denise and Carmody, John. *Religion: The Great Questions* (New York: 1983).

Davies, Brian. *An Introduction to the Philosophy of Religion* (New York: 1982).

Eliade, Mircea. *A History of Religious Ideas*, 2 vols. (Chicago: 1978, 1982).

Ellwood, Robert. *Introducing Religion: From Inside and Outside* (Englewood Cliffs: 1978).

Ellwood, Robert. *Many Peoples, Many Faiths: An Introduction to the Religious Life of Humankind* (Englewood Cliffs: 1982).

Frankl, Viktor. *Man's Search for Meaning* (New York: 1963).

Graham, Aelred. *The End of Religion* (New York: 1971).

Greeley, Andrew. *The Great Mysteries* (New York: 1976).

Heschel, Abraham. *The Wisdom of Heschel* (New York: 1977).

2

Cosmic Riddles: The World of Science

"There is a solution for every problem—simple, neat
. . . and wrong." H.L. Mencken (1880–1956)

The seventeenth century marked a distinctive turning point in human self-understanding. By near universal agreement among historians, it has been accounted the century in which the scientific revolution—often called the Copernican Revolution— began in earnest. This is not to argue necessarily that previous ages were anti-scientific or willfully uninformed, only that the force of events, perceptions and early technologies were changing cosmologies (ways of looking at the universe) by the middle of the 1600's.

Nicholas Copernicus (1473–1543), a Polish astronomer, has his name solidly associated with the shift in thought because it was he who published in 1543 *De Revolutionibus orbium coelestium.* Finished a decade earlier, but delayed in publication, *De Revolutionibus* (and dedicated, incidentally, to Pope Paul III) argued as a hypothesis that the earth moves round the sun, not vice versa as the ancients had held as a near-unanimous opinion, and as common sense supposedly made obvious.

But it was not until the early seventeenth century that the Italian astronomer Galileo Galilei (1564–1642)—born the same year as Shakespeare—was able to substantiate the Copernican thesis with the aid of the technological advance of the telescope. By 1615 the intellectual and clerical world was in an uproar. And what caused so much turmoil? Was it not after all only a question of which bit of celestial real estate gyrated around another? Were the stakes really so high?

High indeed. If Galileo was right, and of course he was, then extraordinary implications followed:

(1) The sages of the past for the most part had been utterly wrong about a fundamental issue: where are we in the universe? Up until this time, the traditional way scholars established certitude on any issue was to refer to the wisdom of the past. Now the ancients had been shown *by scientific evidence* to have made a bad call. Accordingly, part of the modern mind-set took birth at this moment: all things are to be questioned. Everything is up for re-negotiation. Assurance lies not so much in the past as in the present and the future. Not surprisingly, the greatest French philosopher of the century, René Descartes (1596–1650), used universal doubt as his philosophic method, determining that the only thing he could not doubt at the outset of his critical questioning was his own self doubting.

(2) Common sense itself was called into question. The comfortable assurance that, in the physical world at least, things were exactly as they seemed to be, no longer held. The most obvious thing in the world (perhaps literally) had been that the sun moves across the sky as the day wears on. But not so. It only seems so. Recall the bristling moment in *Hamlet* (pub. 1603) when the angry prince snaps at his mother Queen Gertrude: "Seems, madam: Nay it is, I know not seems." (I.2) As another consequence of the work of Copernicus and Galileo, then, much of common sense certitude was undermined.

(3) The easy assumption that humanity was the center of all things in the universe was jolted. And humanity itself, having been in some sense stripped of assurance in its ancient sages, was at one and the same time dethroned from the physical center of the cosmos. At first, it seemed human dignity and destiny itself was at a discount. In *An Anatomie of the World/The First Anniversary*

British poet John Donne (1572–1631) was dismal at the prospect of the new vision of reality:

> And new Philosophy calls all in doubt,
> The element of fire is quite put out.
> The Sun is lost, and the earth, and no mans wit
> Can well direct him where to look for it. . . .
> Tis all in pieces, all coherence gone.

In France, Blaise Pascal (1623–1662) had to confront the same new set of coordinates. In his *Pensées* he wrote:

> On all sides I behold nothing but infinity, in which I am a mere atom, a mere passing shadow that returns no more. All I know is that I must soon die, but what I understand least of all is this very death which I cannot escape.

All coherence, then, seemed gone. The new immensity of things frightened many thinking people who felt like little more than wayward atoms in a void. And yet there was an exhilaration and a headiness to it all.

But by the end of the seventeenth century, if the worlds of religion and philosophy were shaken, the scientist had not yet been enshrined as the new high-priest or philosopher-king. The first reaction to the great revolution, after all, had been that science had given humanity and its destiny quite a drubbing. It had been perceived first not as a liberator, but as a destroyer.

But by 1732 when Alexander Pope (1688–1744) wrote his renowned *Essay on Man,* the situation had changed markedly. Pope was dazzled by the prospect for the newly enlightened human species. He wrote:

> Know then thyself, presume not God to scan;
> The proper study of Mankind is Man.

Placed on this isthmus of a middle state,
A Being darkly wise and rudely great. . . .
The glory, jest and riddle of the world. . . .

Go, wondrous Creature; Mount where Science guides,
Go, measure earth, weigh air, and state the tides;
Instruct the planets in what orbs to run.
Correct old Time, and regulate the Sun.

What had happened in the space of a generation to allow such a generous and highly well-received burst of enthusiasm? What had happened was Sir Isaac Newton (1642–1727), British scientist and the closest thing to a superstar produced by the late seventeenth and early eighteenth centuries. It was Alexander Pope again, in the same *Essay on Man*, who penned the extraordinary lines:

Nature and Nature's laws lay hid in night:
God said, let Newton be: And all was light.

In a study titled simply *The 100*, Michael Hart sets out to rank the most significant figures of history in terms of their impact on their own and later ages. Newton is assigned an amazing *second* place (after Muhammad and before Jesus). People might easily quarrel over such a ranking. But at the very least it is clear that Newton's historical stock, as it were, is extremely high. What was it about this kindly, quiet, pious man that so transformed society and turned science into the undisputed master of the intellectual world for two centuries running?

Quite simply, Newton, by his discoveries of the laws of gravity and motion, was able to establish stability on a grand scale. On both the telescopic and microscopic levels, order and predictability were seen to reign. Whether in the vast reaches of space or on the level of the microbe, an astounding regularity was in evidence.

And not only was it *there,* but humanity could *know* and discover it. There was pattern and consistency across the universe, Newton taught, and the grandeur of the human mind was that it could perceive and predict them. The possibilities, as Alexander Pope was suggesting, seemed limitless. Science was soon being perceived in some quarters at least as the new human savior.

In the nineteenth century, the power and domination of science became ever more obvious to average, even unlettered people. All they had to do was follow the amazing career of science's twin sister, technology. The industrial and transportational uses of steam were quickly changing landscapes, city sizes and life styles. Electricity, the railroad, the telegraph, telephone, electric light, indoor plumbing, anesthetic surgery—all were changing lives, in countless ways and sometimes drastically.

It looked as if centuries of darkness and conflicting theoretical opinions might be drawing to a close as many educated people began to anticipate a new deity for their altar: a divinity whose primary characteristics were facticity, measurement, precision, predictability, and, most important of all, progress. Especially after the work of Charles Darwin (1809–1882)—to be discussed later—the educated world thought itself in a new position with a key to unlock many of the ancient mysteries.

Significantly, by the century's end, it was a scientist such as Germany's Ernst Haeckel (1834–1919) who produced a work with such a sweeping title as *The Riddle of the Universe.* The unknown was, for such a mentality, not a mystery; it was that which was as yet undiscovered.

But the perceptive antennae of the poets and artists were beginning to detect signals of distress even in the nineteenth century. All was not well in the new religion of scientific certitude; it was no more explaining complexity and mystery in simple and uniform ways than were the earlier and older faiths. What's more, the new mood and method were concentrating on only one aspect of reality to the exclusion of others, distorting the human picture.

Charles Dickens (1812–1870) sensed all of this as early as 1854 in his stinging portrayal in *Hard Times* of Mr. Gradgrind, a teacher whose impoverished world is defined by facts alone, only and always facts.

Alfred Tennyson (1809–1892) wrote *In Memoriam* in 1850, a poem that bristled with the conflict of the old and new faiths:

> O yet we trust that somehow good
> Will be the final goal of ill,
> To pangs of nature, sins of will,
> Defects of doubt and taints of blood;
>
> That nothing walks with aimless feet;
> That not one life shall be destroyed,
> Or cast as rubbish to the void
> When God hath made the pile complete. . . .
>
> Behold we know not anything;
> I can but trust that good shall fall
> At last—far off—at last, to all,
> And every winter change to spring.
>
> So runs my dream: but what am I?
> An infant crying in the night
> An infant crying for the light,
> And with no language but a cry. . . .
>
> Are God and Nature then at strife,
> That Nature lends such evil dreams?
> So careful of the type she seems
> So careless of the single life
>
> That I, considering everywhere
> Her secret meaning in her deeds,
> And finding that of fifty seeds
> She often brings but one to bear,

I falter where I firmly trod,
And falling with my weight of cares
Upon the great world's altar-stairs
That slope through darkness up to God,

I stretch lame hands of faith and grope,
And gather dust and chaff, and call,
To what I feel is Lord of all,
And faintly trust the larger hope. . . .

And in 1867, another British poet, Matthew Arnold (1822–1888), concluded "Dover Beach" with this chilling assessment:

. . . for the world which seems
To lie before us, like a land of dreams,
So various, so beautiful, so new,
Hath really neither joy, nor love, nor light,
Nor certitude, nor peace, nor help for pain
And we are here as on a darkling plain
Swept with confused alarms of struggle and flight
Where ignorant armies clash by night.

By the 1890's, an even more profound unsettlement had set in among scientists themselves, and by the early years of the twentieth century it was possible to speak of "a second scientific revolution." What was happening, after the work of Marie Curie (1867–1934), Ernest Rutherford (1871–1937), Niels Bohr (1885–1962), Max Planck (1858–1947) and Albert Einstein (1879–1955), was that certitude and stability were being replaced as reigning concepts by probability, relativity, and, in the word of Werner Heisenberg (b. 1901), indeterminacy.

Put another way, in the words of Michael Biddiss in a very fine essay in *The Age of the Masses: Ideas and Society in Europe Since 1870*, "the atom—derived from the Greek for 'indivisible'—could no longer live up to its name. Indeed, inquiry into the nature of disintegration within atoms was to be a central theme of the new physics now emerging.'' The basic presumption of classical physics that continuity is present in all the causal situations of nature was now being replaced by a quantum physics that described energy emitted discontinuously.

None of this meant, of course, that science was dethroned or that the great search for cosmic coherence carried out by an Einstein or a Freud was in vain. It did mean, though, that the world of science began to realize its own limitations, its dependence upon relative models of the structure of reality.

In 1977 Ronald Duncan and Miranda Weston Smith published an *Encyclopedia of Ignorance* with articles from such famous scientists as Linus Pauling and Francis Crick detailing the staggering amount of information science does not now or possibly never will know. This unique encyclopedia gives evidence that we often do not even recognize the scope of our ignorance. Not only do we not have answers; we sometimes haven't formulated good questions.

Surveying the changed intellectual and scientific scene, Alan Watts commented in *The Wisdom of Insecurity* that the centuries-old struggle between science and religion had not ended with the result that religion was false and science was true. Rather, he wrote, ''All systems of definition are relative to various purposes; none of them actually 'grasp' reality.''

Furthermore, Watts continued, the world of science was safe and dependable on its own grounds of matter, energy, motion, number, theory and structure. But science went awry when it tried to account for all reality.

> The heart has learned to feel that we live for the future. Science may, slowly and uncertainly, give us a better future—for a few years. And then, for each of us, it will end. However long postponed, everything composed must decompose.

Not only had it become apparent that science was not omniscient or omnicompetent: it also had a shadow side. Exploding knowledge had brought exhilarating new conceptualizations and excellent advances in medicine, transportation, technology and life style. But it brought a bitter harvest as well. Industrialization brought with it the explosive growth of cities. With such cities came slums, corruption, and eroding family structures. Technology also gave rise to new ways of polluting the atmosphere, of turning the worker into a mere small cog in a very large operation. And it yielded after the summer of 1945 the nuclear age that carries with it the threat of destruction of all living forms on the planet. Jonathan Schell's *The Fate of the Earth* traces in careful detail the scientific explanation of the splitting of the atom, its use in weapons systems, and the current capability of total earth destruction. Schell quotes such steady voices as that of Henry Kissinger warning about humanity's possibility of destroying itself and Jimmy Carter's fear that civilization is now in a position to commit suicide.

So far, this chapter has set out to make two points:

(1) Science, which came to assume a major intellectual leadership in the early modern period, had by the mid-twentieth century undergone a time of trial and chastening. This is certainly not to diminish the importance or the dignity of scientific method; it is only to say that science has come to learn its own limitations. The same point will be made about the major western religious traditions in a later chapter.

(2) In addition to a series of technological blessings that science has helped to bestow upon humanity, it has also bequeathed a legacy of problems, fears and extreme and very present dangers.

One third, last point needs to be made before the end of the current discussion of natural science and the ultimate questions. While it is true that the scientific method has not proven to be competent to take all the great mysteries within its ken, it is also true that twentieth century science has been a primary pointer to the enduring mysteries of human history.

To look into any contemporary text in physics or astronomy is to get a glimpse of exotic, mind-bending, ultimate considerations. What is matter after all? And what is the universe? Are there many universes? What existed before creation? Did matter always exist? Did a primal "big bang" explosion of hydrogen atoms cast the whole cosmic process out into limitless space? Or is space curved and will the process collapse back on itself and begin again?

And what about *black holes*? As a reviewer in the *New York Review of Books* noted:

> Since 1960 the universe has taken on a wholly new face. It has become more exciting, more mysterious, more violent, and more extreme as our knowledge concerning it has suddenly expanded. And the most exciting, most mysterious, most violent and most extreme phenomenon of all has the simplest, plainest, calmest and mildest name—nothing more than a black hole.

Black holes are assumed to be vast spaceless gaps into which atomic particles and suns disappear without leaving traces. A star's matter can end by being crushed utterly out of existence.

As *Time* magazine (September 4, 1978) in a feature on black holes noted:

> Black holes are rips in the very fabric of space and time, places where long-cherished laws of nature simply do not apply. . . . If whole stars can literally vanish from sight within black holes, literally crushed out of existence, where has their matter gone? To another place and another time? Where did it come from? In searching for answers to these fundamental questions raised by black holes, scientists are infringing on

the realm of philosophers and theologians. They are trying to find out the meaning of life, of being, of the universe.

Surely even some of the most abstruse argumentation of the philosophers, the murkiest dogmatic hassles of the theologians sound tame compared to the working terminology of late twentieth century astronomers. The "riddle of the universe" becomes more, not less, intricate.

And if modern astronomy forces us to acknowledge *intricacy,* it also would have us face up to *immensity.* Vastness in the universe of itself establishes nothing. But it casts us into a sobering framework in which to contemplate questions of even deeper significance than size. One doesn't need to agree with all the presuppositions of a Carl Sagan to appreciate his conciseness in describing our situation in his book *Cosmos:*

> We live on a mote of dust circling a humdrum star in the remotest corner of an obscure galaxy. And if we are a speck in the immensity of space, we also occupy an instant in the expanse of the ages. We now know that our universe, or at least its most recent incarnation, is some 15 or 20 billion years old.
>
> A galaxy is composed of gas and dust and stars—billions upon billions of stars. Each star may be a sun to someone. Within each galaxy there are stars and worlds, and it may be, a proliferation of living things and intelligent beings and space-faring civilizations. . . . There are some hundred billion galaxies (10^{11}) each with, on the average, a hundred billion stars. In all the galaxies, there are perhaps as many planets as stars, 10 billion trillion (10^{22}).

The cosmic riddle will not go quietly away. It is not just something outside us to ponder from time to time. We carry the great mysteries around in our bodies and our organs, our emotions, our minds. The world of science doesn't solve these mysteries for us. It makes them more evident, more compelling, more seductive. The mystery of it all is, in fact, a lure to mystic and scientist alike.

Further Reading

Biddiss, Michael. *The Age of the Masses: Ideas and Society in Europe Since 1870* (New York: 1977).

Brinton, Crane. *The Shaping of Modern Thought* (New York: 1963).

Capra, Fritjof. *The Tao of Physics* (New York: 1978).

Jastrow, R. *God and the Astronomers* (New York: 1978).

Johnson, Paul. *Modern Times* (New York: 1983).

Nebelsick, Harold. *Theology and Science in Mutual Modification* (New York: 1981).

Randall, John H. *The Making of the Modern Mind* (Cambridge: 1940).

Schilling, Harold. *The New Consciousness in Science and Religion* (Philadelphia: 1973).

Wilford, John Noble. ''To the Edge of the Universe: The New Age of Astronomy'' in *New York Times Magazine* (September 15, 1985).

3

Telling the Human Story:
Literature

"No one is happy all of life long."
Euripides (480–406 B.C.)

One of the oldest and deepest of human passions is the need to tell stories, and to hear them. Our romance with the tale, the myth, the epic, the yarn is tied in with our fascination and reverence for the *word*. Not only are we the animals who wonder why; we are creatures who talk, who have developed an intricate system of communication symbols to transmit a vast range of ideas, facts, emotions, and intuitions.

Words are shaping-realities. Words are power. Quite literally, the word can be mightier than the sword, the bullet or the bomb. And the power of the word can be used for good or for evil. In personal dealings we can use words to encourage and support others; or we can use words to sting, to deceive and to devastate.

Politically, words carry with them an impact of unbelievable consequences. Consider the oratory of Churchill over the BBC in 1940. England had every physical, psychological and military reason to fall apart at that stage in the Second World War. But it was in good measure Churchill's bulldog prose that saved, sustained and shaped a nation for survival. And with his words, Churchill told them a story about who the British people had been, and what they must be again.

Hitler, too, effectively used the word in his rise to power in the troubled Germany of the 1930's. At an early stage of his career, if he had gone house to house with armed men to spread his message, people might have resisted. But they did not resist his word, his message—again, a story about the German people, who they had been, and what had been done to them.

Whether it is on this great international cosmic scale, or the personal level of what our companions say to us each day, words help to control attitudes, moods, even civilizations. Words shape, tell a story; they also can be a glory in themselves, a work of wrought beauty as stunning as tides and cliffs and eclipses that compel us to watch them for the sake of wonder alone.

Great literature has in good part been defined by its ability to portray great characters, protagonists, humanists and villains as they confront the primal emotions and the ultimate questions. It is precisely because of such portrayals that world literature is included in practically all the core curricula of colleges and universities. From Homer to Chaucer to Shakespeare, from Dostoevsky to Emily Dickinson to Saul Bellow, great writers have been seekers, and partial finders, of fundamental insights about the mystery of human life.

And while we are still by all accounts a linear-literate people, we also find the fascination with primal things in our generation emerging in art forms unknown to earlier generations: the film and the rock idiom in particular. A careful listening and informed viewing will convince us that these are not only entertainment media; if they are worthy of their medium, they also are seriously committed to telling aspects of the human story.

What continues in this chapter will be but a collection of passages from often well-known literary pieces with only the briefest word of introduction. Their purpose is to provide a few models of the mixture of the thinker's perception and the writer's skill as they come to bear on the ultimate things. A careful reading of these passages will also enable the reader to hear again the notes sounded in the first chapter—themes of primal human concern: purpose, meaning, divinity, pain, hope, character, resources and morality.

William Shakespeare (1564–1616)

In the English-speaking world, only the Bible competes with Shakespeare as the fundamental source of insight into the human condition. The following selections, perhaps the best known of all the Bard's passages, provide us with one of Shakespeare's voices, surely one of his most profound. In the first selection from *Macbeth* (Act V, Scene 5), Shakespeare leads with an attempt to define, in shortest compass, the meaning of life itself.

Tomorrow and tomorrow and tomorrow
Creeps in this petty pace from day to day
To the last syllable of recorded time;
And all our yesterdays have lighted fools
The way to dusty death. Out, out brief candle!
Life's but a walking shadow, a poor player,
That struts and frets his hour upon the stage
And then is heard no more. It is a tale
Told by an idiot, full of sound and fury,
Signifying nothing.

In the second piece, from *Hamlet* (Act III, Scene 1), he puzzles over life's ever present companion, death.

To be, or not to be, that is the question.
Whether tis nobler in the mind to suffer
The slings and arrows of outrageous fortune,
Or to take arms against a sea of troubles,
And by opposing them, end them. To die, to sleep
No more, and by a sleep to say we end
The heart-ache, and the thousand natural shocks
That flesh is heir to; tis a consummation
Devoutly to be wished. . . .

For who would bear the whips and scorns of time,
The oppressor's wrong, the proud man's contumely,
The pangs of disprized loves, the law's delay,
The insolence of office, and the spurns
That patient merit of th' unworthy takes,
When he himself might his quietus make
With a bare bodkin. . . .

But that the dread of something after death,
The undiscovered country, from whose bourn
No traveller returns, puzzles the will,
And makes us rather bear those ills we have,
Than fly to others we know not of?
The conscience does make cowards of us all.

Albert Camus (1913–1960)

A prominent French existentialist, practically a cult figure for countless American youth of the 1960's generation, Camus puzzled over the sense of absurdity so often printed on life itself. In the center of all life's murkiness, he labored to find that which was worthy of mature effort and heroic resistance to what he considered the void. Camus, who could speak of finding a surprising spring in the midst of a personal winter, wrote *La Peste* (*The Plague*) in 1947 with a heroic doctor fighting against pestilence as its central figure. Near the conclusion, Camus, struggling to give his Dr. Rieux a ground for his good efforts, wrote that he wanted

> . . . to state quite simply what we learn in time of pestilence; that there are more things to admire in men than to despise.
>
> Nevertheless (Dr. Rieux) knew that the tale he had to tell could not be one of a final victory. It could only be the record of what had to be done and what assuredly would have to be

done again in the never ending fight against terror and its relentless onslaughts, despite their personal afflictions by all who, unable to be saints, but refusing to bow down to pestilences, strive their utmost to be healers.

Fyodor Dostoevsky (1821–1881)

In his great masterpiece from 1880, *The Brothers Karamazov*, this Russian novelist provided a stunning canvas of anguished moderns, seeking faith in themselves, in the world and in God in the midst of the eroding stabilities of the past. The brothers Ivan and Alyosha offer contrasting, often conflicting approaches to life as the story unfolds. But at the very conclusion, Dostoevsky offers a kind of hymn to the possibility for goodness printed irreducibly in each human heart. A neighborhood boy, Ilusha, has died. Alyosha speaks to the other boys of the area:

> Let us make a compact, here at Ilusha's stone that we will never forget Ilusha and one another. And whatever happens to us later in life . . . let us always remember how we buried the poor boy at whom we threw stones, do you remember, by the bridge? And afterwards we all grew so fond of him. He was a fine boy, a kind-hearted, brave boy. . . . And even if we are occupied with more important things, if we attain to honor, or fall into misfortune, still let us remember how good it once was here, when we were all together, united by a kind and good feeling which made us, for the time we were loving that poor boy, better perhaps than we are. . . .

> You must know that there is nothing higher and stronger and more wholesome for good in life than some good memory. . . .

Emily Dickinson (1830–1886)

With many of the American writers, such as Emily Dickinson, there is to be found an intensive search for significance in the seemingly insignificant, the extraordinary in the ordinary. Miss Dickinson, the ''Belle of Amherst,'' lived a secluded life in inner Massachusetts.

> The brain is wider than the sky—
> For—put them side by side—
> The one the other will contain
> With ease—and You—beside.

> The Brain is deeper than the sea—
> For—hold them—Blue to blue—
> The one the other will absorb—
> As Sponges—Buckets—do.

> The brain is just the weight of God—
> For—Heft them—Pound for pound—
> And they will differ—if they do—
> As Syllable from sound.

. . . .

> To venerate the simple days
> Which lead the seasons by,
> Needs but to remember
> That from you and I,
> They may take the trifle
> Termed mortality.

. . . .

> For each ecstatic instant
> We must an anguish pay
> In keen and quivering ratio
> To the ecstasy.

> For each beloved hour
> Sharp pittances of years,
> Bitter contested farthings
> And coffers heaped with tears.

. . . .

Tell the truth, but tell it slant,
The truth must dazzle gradually,
Or every eye be blind.
. . . .
I know that He exists.
Somewhere—in silence—
He has hid his rare life
From our gross eyes.
. . . .
This World is not Conclusion.
A Species stands beyond—
Invisible as music—
But positive as sound—
It beckons and it baffles—
Philosophy—don't know—
And through a Riddle, at the Last
Sagacity must go—
To guess it, puzzles scholars—
To gain it, Men have borne
Contempt of generations
And Crucifixion shown—
Faith slips and laughs and rallies—
Blushes if any see
Plucks at a twig of Evidence—
And asks a Vane the way,
Much Gesture from the Pulpit—
Strong hallelujahs roll—
Narcotics cannot still the Tooth
That nibbles at the soul.

Thornton Wilder (b. 1897)

Along with Edgar Lee Masters, Sherwood Anderson and
Sinclair Lewis, Wilder found his themes and personalities in
small-town America. While many contemporary twentieth century Americans began to feel that one wasn't somehow in the

mainstream of life without being in the whirl of New York or Chicago or Los Angeles, Wilder and his colleagues found the whole wide range of the human heart in any hamlet big enough at least to sustain the high dignity of a county seat. In *Our Town,* the recently deceased Emily spends a day back on earth and muses on her return to the cemetery:

I didn't realize. So all that was going on and we never noticed. Take me back—up the hill—to my grave. But first: Wait! One more look.
Good-by, Good-by, world. Good-by, Grover's Corners . . . Mama and Papa. Good-by to clocks ticking . . . and Mama's sunflowers. And food and coffee. And new-ironed dresses and hot baths . . . and sleeping and waking up. Oh, earth, you're too wonderful for anybody to realize you.
She looks toward the stage manager and asks abruptly, through her tears:
Do any human beings ever realize life while they live it?— every, every minute?

Edgar Lee Masters (1869–1950)

Masters, another chronicler of the vast world in the small town, created *Spoon River Anthology,* a shocking book when it appeared in 1915. Based on his own early life in the towns of Petersburg and Lewistown, Illinois, the work is made up of 244 very brief autobiographies revealing the secret lives and feelings of the citizenry. Some are revealed as hidden sinners, others as hidden saints. Included here are two selections showing, in the Widow McFarlane a kind of desperation with life, and in Lucinda Matlock (probably based on Masters' own grandmother) an enduring love of it.

Widow McFarlane

I was the Widow McFarlane,
Weaver of carpets for all the village.
And I pity you still at the loom of life,
You who are singing to the shuttle
And lovingly watching the work of your hands,
If you reach the day of hate, of terrible truth.
For the cloth of life is woven, you know,
To a pattern hidden under the loom—
A pattern you never see!
And you weave high-hearted, singing, singing,
You guard the threads of love and friendship
For noble figures in gold and purple.
And long after other eyes can see
You have woven a moon-white strip of cloth
You laugh in your strength, for Hope o'erlays it
With shapes of love and beauty.
The loom stops short! The pattern's out!
You're alone in the room! You have woven a shroud!
And hate of it lays you in it!

Lucinda Matlock

I went to the dances at Chandlerville,
And played snap-out at Winchester.
One time we changed partners,
Driving home in the moonlight of middle June,
And then I found Davis.
We were married and lived together for seventy years,
Enjoying working, raising the twelve children,
Eight of whom we lost
Ere I had reached the age of sixty.
I spun, I wove, I kept the house, I nursed the sick,
I made the garden, and for holiday
Rambled over the fields where sang the larks,

And by Spoon River gathering many a shell,
And many a flower and medicinal weed—
Shouting to the wooded hills, singing to the green valleys.
At ninety-six I had lived enough, that is all,
And passed to a sweet repose.
What is this I hear of sorrow and weariness,
Anger, discontent and drooping hopes?
Degenerate sons and daughters,
Life is too strong for you—
It takes life to love Life.

The selections from American literature could go on, of course, at length. The works of such classic writers as Hemingway, Fitzgerald and Faulkner are laden with the questions of human relationship and significance. Among post-war and more recent authors, the questioning, troubling complexities and insights continue in the writing of such figures as Donald Bartheleme, Saul Bellow, Raymond Carver, John Cheever, Bobbie Ann Mason, Flannery O'Connor, Isaac Bashevis Singer, John Updike, Kurt Vonnegut and Eudora Welty.

Further Reading

Berger, Peter. *The Heretical Imperative: Contemporary Possibilities of Religious Affirmation* (New York: 1979).
Bettelheim, Bruno. *The Uses of Enchantment* (New York: 1977).
Dunne, John. *The Way of All the Earth* (New York: 1972).
Fowler, James. *Stages of Faith* (San Francisco: 1981).
McClendon, James. *Biography as Theology* (Nashville: 1974).
Shea, John. *Stories of God: An Unauthorized Biography* (Chicago: 1974).
Tracy, David. *Blessed Rage for Order* (New York: 1975).

4

A Schizoid World:
The Social Sciences

"The real tragedy of life is what dies inside a man
while he still lives."
Albert Schweitzer (1875–1965)

Rollo May, one of the most noted of living American psychologists, gives an excellent example in his best-selling
book *Love and Will* of the closeness of the psychological sciences
to the traditional ultimate considerations. May is thoroughly familiar with the great issues of religion, science, philosophy and
psychology, and in *Love and Will*, as well as in his other books
such as *The Meaning of Anxiety*, he constantly interrelates them
all.

In briefly reviewing *Love and Will* here and offering some
excerpts, the purpose is not to urge Rollo May as a final word in
any of these academic areas. Rather, it is to show that, however
one might personally decide such issues, the world of psychology
in particular and the social sciences in general are truly a most
fertile ground for the consideration of ultimate questions.

Love and Will opens with an unsettling, yet carefully reasoned essay titled "Our Schizoid World." It is not a very pretty
designation for something so complicated as a world.

Schizoid, after all, means out of touch; avoiding close con-
tact; having lost the ability to feel. It suggests isolation, withdrawal and loneliness. How does May make his case by applying
such terms not just to a few troubled individuals, but to a society
as a whole?

Building on the work of existential philosophers and theologians, as well as his own clinical practice, May describes *anxiety* as the central problem of our time. It will be our collective responses to such anxiety, he maintains, that will precipitate the schizoid state.

Anxiety is a pervasive fear in life that has no particular object. It is not so much a specific fear such as that of crowds, or small places, or flying, or spiders that can be handled to some extent by avoiding their occasions. Anxiety is much more deep-seated and not nearly so easy to escape. It involves a sense of something impending over us, and that something is not anything good. Life starts to be lived on the defensive, under a cloud. Not only are more people coming to professionals with such feelings; our artists have sensed it as well. Auden wrote "The Age of Anxiety" and Leonard Bernstein has composed a "Symphony for the Age of Anxiety." Such social thinkers as Christopher Lasch have written about our anxious age (*Haven in a Heartless World*), as have Alvin Toffler (*Future Shock*), Robert Heilbroner (*An Inquiry into the Human Prospect*) and Jonathan Schell in the previously mentioned *The Fate of the Earth*.

How do we account for so much anxiety in the late twentieth century, especially in America? The reasons are not far to seek. Several modern commentators have spoken about them, and we provide only a sketch of a listing here:

1. *Nuclear Weapons*. First on practically everyone's listing is the apocalyptic reality of the existence of a nuclear arsenal in the world since 1945. Its might is now such that the capability is already present for obliterating all living forms from the earth.

2. *Competitiveness*. Technology, computerization and the pace of "future shock" are constituting an extremely sophisticated market, work force, and service-oriented economy. The competitiveness necessary to keep on top of these situations, coupled with the deep-seated American drive to excel and to succeed, has caught up vast numbers into a life style of tension, insecurity,

workaholism, and sometimes of early strokes, heart attacks and nervous disorders.

3. *Exaggerated Expectations*. Fired by advertising, film and peer pressures, Americans often revere extremes of size, wealth, and beauty; they seemingly cannot forgive themselves if they do not measure up to such top-of-the-line realities. Often the culture pushes for perfection, especially self-perfection and actualization *now*. People discover all too late—or not at all—that their emotional and achievement agenda are being set outside themselves, and sometimes at the expense of both others and themselves. One more ground for anxiety and pressure.

4. *Mobility*. Just as some levels of competition and high expectations are healthy for individuals and societies, so is the freedom of change and mobility. But once again, commentators have been quick to point out that the United States has made practically a fetish of mobility whether in one's residence or occupation or across the landscape. The average U.S. citizen is said to change housing about every fifth year. We leap into our cars and go anywhere at once at the slightest provocation. Graduating high school students expect to have perhaps a series of careers or professions in a lifetime. There are certain benefits to all these things, of course, but there are also prices to pay. The constant change of domicile leads to a lack of rootedness, and to the erosion of family and friendship linkages that shape and even define individual lives.

5. *Lack of Religious Center*. Increasingly western people find it difficult to define for themselves a common core of beliefs and values. Religion, long a leader in the formation of such definitions, continues to have a power and vitality; yet it may well continue to experience a diminished centrality in the lives of ever more persons in a secularized culture. So it is that yet one more factor that once helped provide stability, purpose, and shape to a life has been eclipsed for many individuals, and anxieties rise apace.

How do people respond to the all-too-evident fact of anxiety in life? According to Rollo May, there are two widely divergent responses. The first, very tempting alternative is at the same time quite unhealthy; it is the path of apathy. The second, healthy, integrated approach is that of creativity that effectively reactivates the human capacities of love and will.

All too many moderns respond to anxiety, May believes, by avoidance and denial. They turn to indifference and non-involvement to shield themselves from formless, threatening twentieth century life. In the process, they turn more and more in upon themselves, become a "me-generation," and assume they have attained a kind of safety zone. What they have really reached, again, according to May, is an even greater level of dangers. These dangers include a less-than-human isolationism, an apathy that leads to powerlessness, a vacuum of leadership, and finally a situation in which others take control. The stage is set for frustration, anger, and violence.

The other approach to dealing with anxiety involves a kind of fundamental recasting of a life—an acceptance of life with what Lutheran theologian Paul Tillich (a friend of Rollo May) had called "the courage to be." This second approach leads the individual to face the anxieties and crises not only as obstacles, but as opportunities—for creativity, for forging a true self-identity, for compassion, for inner development. The key words in this process are deceptively simple: love and will. As a culture, we have, May believes, nearly forgotten their meaning.

If the problems are essentially anxiety, emptiness, loneliness, isolation, then the solutions can only be the *linkage* of individuals to wider worlds of emotional, intellectual, personal, community, and spiritual involvement. An individual or a society that is out of touch desperately needs *bridges,* and these are primarily through intellect, will and emotion. It is hardly an accident that these bridges parallel the three classic virtues of Christianity: faith, hope and love.

Ironically, May thinks, this is an age that needs love in the deepest way, yet it has come to settle for sex without love or emotional involvement as one of its main hallmarks. People today, May announces in a blunt judgment, are having sex more but enjoying it less. We are entering, he says, a new age of Puritanism in which the body is split off from the rest of our affections, and viewed and treated primarily as a machine. Sex, which can be a most profound human, emotional, spiritual involvement, has in effect been diminished to a mechanical event, ruled by manual and the same impossible expectations that strain so much else in modern living.

Casual sex, May concludes, is harmful primarily because it undercuts the very intensity and power of what sex itself ought to be. It not only links individuals in strength and vulnerability and tenderness, but it also enables men and women to partake in a primal pulsation of the cosmos, of life, of creation itself. Divorced from these greater realities, sexuality turns into ''glandular hydraulics.'' By depersonalizing the sexual, twentieth century types have taken the fig leaf off the genitals in their statues (which the Victorians had placed there in their repressiveness) only to move it to the face.

For the sake of sex itself and the sake of humanity, then, our society needs to be more *erotic* in the full sense of the term. More mere sexiness and ''cute'' use of bodies in ads and on screens we do not need. That kind of sexiness is, again, the new Puritanism. Eros, May reminds the reader, is a yearning for wholeness, relatedness and integration. Genital sexuality is part of this wider truth. To reduce sexuality to tension-release alone would only reinforce the ultimately self-destructive selfishness that cares only about one's immediate physical feelings.

> To act on emotion and feeling alone is to inhabit a radically solipsistic (only the self is ultimately real) system. It leaves us separated like monads, alienated, with no bridge to any

persons around us. We can "emote" and have sexual relations till doomsday and never experience any real relationship with another person.

Ultimately, one does not lose one's identity in humane sexuality. Rather, other-love invites genuine self-worth. As psychologist Harry Stack Sullivan insists, we love others to the extent that we are capable of loving ourselves. Eros is, according to May, the center and vitality of a person and a culture. Without eros they revert to a kind of living death, the second of Freud's eros/thanatos options (to be discussed later). The opposite of eros is thanatos, coldness, death.

Love and death are strangely linked together, as all the major psychologists (as well as Woody Allen) have observed. May quotes Abraham Maslow: "I wonder if we could love passionately, if ecstasy would be possible, if we knew we would never die."

There is a way in which couples in love die to self and give themselves over in the most open emotional vulnerability to the other. Genuine sexuality, as May describes it, draws one ecstatically out of the self; and that, too, is a kind of death to an older and isolated self.

Love is not only linked to a certain loss of self. It is also linked to "the daimonic." As Rollo May explains this concept, it is complicated, difficult to grasp; yet, it is vital. And it is not to be simply confused with the demonic or diabolical. The daimonic, as he presents it, is any natural function which has the power to take over the whole person. It is an urge to affirm and expand the self.

In its right proportion, the daimonic is the urge to reach out toward others, to increase life by way of sex, to create, to civilize; it is the joy and rapture, or the simple security of knowing, that we can affect others, can form them, can exert power which is demonstrably significant. It is a way of making certain that we are valued.

The daimonic, of course, because it is powerful, also needs check points and accountabilities. These include dialogue, self-criticism and possibilities for new integration of experience.

The understanding of the will, no less than that of love, has been diminished and crippled in our time, May writes. And if we are not as a race possessed of the full range of inner freedoms we once thought we had, neither are we locked into a total determinism; we maintain some intimate areas of choice and action within ourselves. Complete determinists run up against a contradiction in their own argumentation, says May. If there are no standards for right and wrong, if all things are merely determined to be as such, then even determinists may not argue their positions as right, but only that they are determined to hold such positions. A therapist must act on the presumption of at least some minimal basis of the patient's freedom, or else that same psychologist could never urge treatment or change on a patient.

> Man is determined by his capacity to know that he is determined and to choose his relationship to what determines him. . . . The first act of freedom is to choose it.

Will is the capacity to organize one's self so that movement toward a defined goal can take place. Linked to will is intentionality—the human capacity to have intentions in the first place. Intentionality is a "bridge between extremes of subjectivism and objectivism. Intention is a stretching toward something . . . a dynamism . . . it involves commitment."

Perhaps most importantly for Rollo May, will and intentionality are pointers to the fact that there is more to the world than brute facticity. The words "I can" or "I can't" point to intensely real experiences in life.

Both love and will are forms of experience that show the human person reaching out to touch others and in the process being touched in return. The will can block love by manipulation; love can block the will by permissiveness.

The central need of the age, then, the main antidote to anxiety, is a blending of love and will that can be summed up in the German word *Sorge*—in English, care:

> Care is the refusal to accept emptiness, though it face one on every side.
> Care is the dogged insistence on human dignity, though it be violated on every side.
> Care is the stubborn assertion of the self to give content to our activities, routine though they be.

By his study of such psychological controversies as love, will, freedom, determinism, eros, intentionality and the daimonic, Rollo May has provided a textbook example of the reach of ultimate questions into the social sciences. To reiterate, even if one disagrees in a major way with his conclusions or his comments along the way, one cannot help but realize the profound social, cultural and political consequences of those elusive, yet ever present mysteries we keep calling the ultimate questions.

Further Reading

Bellah, Robert, *et al. Habits of the Heart* (Berkeley: 1985).

Cox, Harvey. *Religion in the Secular City* (New York: 1984).

Hodgson, Godfrey. *American in Our Time: From World War II to Nixon* (New York: 1978).

Lasch, Christopher. *The Culture of Narcissism: American Life in an Age of Diminishing Expectations* (New York: 1979).

May, Rollo. *The Meaning of Anxiety* (New York: 1977).

O'Neill, William. *Coming Apart: An Informal History of America in the 1960's* (New York: 1977).

Slater, Philip. *The Pursuit of Loneliness: American Culture at the Breaking Point* (New York: 1970).

Tillich, Paul. *The Courage To Be* (New York: 1952).

Tracy, David. *The Analogical Imagination* (New York: 1981).

Unit Two:

Thoughtful Responses

5

The Foundations Shake

"Courage is the resistance to fear . . . not the absence of it."
Mark Twain (1835–1910)

C hapter Two of this text set about to describe in very summary fashion the shift in scientific world view from the seventeenth century down to our own that brought us into what is generally described as "modern consciousness." The purpose of the present chapter is to examine the thought of three thinkers who lived in the nineteenth century whose works were immensely influential on the formation of new world views. Each in his own way—Marx, Darwin, and Freud—caused the old established foundations to shake by providing new, largely non-religious lenses through which to gaze at a comprehensive picture of human life and its destiny.

For those in love with the status quo, the late eighteenth and nineteenth centuries were a particularly jolting time in which to live. In ever so many areas, the old established order seemed to crumble into dust.

Politically, the late eighteenth century witnessed the American and the French Revolutions with their insistences on fundamental human rights, and a limitation of governmental authority based on the proposition that the right to rule derives from the consent of the governed. For sheer bravado there can be few lines in history more extraordinary than Jefferson's in the 1776 Declaration of Independence:

> We hold these truths to be self-evident, that all men are cre-
> ated equal, that they are endowed by their Creator with cer-
> tain unalienable Rights, that among these are Life, Liberty
> and the pursuit of Happiness. That to secure these rights,
> Governments are instituted among Men, deriving their just
> powers from the consent of the governed.

Self-evident! Generations, centuries and millennia had held
largely the opposite and based their structures of governance on
an assumed and unbridgeable inequality.

The American experience with fundamental liberties was one
historical thing, the French experience quite something else as the
Revolution became the Terror. The early nineteenth century in
Europe was in large part the story of reaction to liberties run wild
in Paris in 1793.

Technologically, the century was a marvel. The steamboat,
the steam locomotive, telegraph and telephone revolutionized
travel and communication. Advances in electricity, photography,
phonography, medicine, surgery; the growth of industry, cities,
transatlantic immigration—all these changed lives drastically for
the millions.

The century soon began to identify itself as the "Age of
Progress," especially after the Crystal Palace Exhibition in London in 1851 and the Centennial Exhibition in Philadelphia in
1876. Perhaps most incredible and melancholy of all, the century
even began to think of itself as wonderfully progressive in human
relations. From the Congress of Vienna (1815) to the onset of the
First World War (1914) there was little by way of global warfare
as earlier centuries had known. In fact, the Crimean War for Brit-
ain (1853–1856) and the Civil War for the United States (1861–
1865) were among the few really massive and extended battle situations of the age. There were those thinkers who began to think
that serious wars were part of humanity's past, swept aside by the
drive of inevitable progress.

In philosophy, as we have already seen, radical doubt had been very much the order of the day from Descartes on. Then, in the century of Enlightenment itself, little could have been more shocking than the work of David Hume (1711–1776) who threw into question the certainty of causality, one of the very grounds of Enlightenment natural science. Immanuel Kant (1724–1804), the great German philosopher, "awakened from his dogmatic slumbers" by the Scotsman Hume, developed what he considered a philosophic revolution parallel in significance to that of Copernicus in astronomy. Kant maintained that we can never know the reality-in-itself (noumenon) with certitude, but only the thing as it presents itself to our appearance (phenomenon). Truth was not so much, for Kant, conformity of our minds to things, as the conformity of things to the categories of our mind's understanding capacities.

Georg Hegel (1770–1831), yet another German thinker, created a revolution of his own by insisting that reality is not so much ultimately changeless, stable and timeless. Rather, reality should be seen as changing, tumultuous, conflictual. Absolute Spirit moves through history not in abstractions, but is involved deeply in exchange and turmoil. The process by which the Spirit moves is Hegel's famous threefold dialectic: *thesis* which interacts with its opposing *antithesis* to produce *synthesis* which in turn becomes a new thesis. And the cycle goes on without end. This philosophic viewing of reality as dynamic would have very important influences on Marx in particular. Practically no great thinker of the age was untouched by Hegel's thought.

In the world of religion, Christianity had to come to grips with two decidedly new factors: (1) the development, beginning in Germany, of critical biblical scholarship that was becoming known on the public, non-scholarly level as early as the 1830's; (2) the growing awareness of the writings and beliefs of many major world religions, especially in the 1880's.

Onto this scene, already electrified, as it were, by new revelations from the natural sciences, were to come three thinkers whose names would become household words. Their thoughts and theories, their ways of coming to grips with the ultimate questions, would make the nineteenth century more intensely than ever a time of the shaking of the foundations.

Taking a lead from a very useful, short book by Leslie Stevenson, *Seven Theories of Human Nature,* our brief examination of the three thinkers, as well as of some others in the next chapter, will proceed through a fourfold method.

Of each thinker we will pose the questions:

(1) What is the nature of the universe?
(2) How does humanity fit into this picture?
(3) What is the fundamental flaw in the human situation?
(4) What, if any, is the remedy for this flaw?

Charles Darwin (1809–1882)

English naturalist Charles Darwin, the grandson of botanist and poet Erasmus Darwin, studied at different times in his life to be a physician and a clergyman. He settled into neither profession, but instead his seminal work would influence the clerical, medical and scientific worlds ever after.

Darwin was born, half a planet away, on the very same day as Abraham Lincoln. There have not been lacking those commentators who point out that as Lincoln freed the American slave, so did Darwin deliver biology up from its historic dogmatisms. Such earth-shaking as Darwin did, he accomplished after a five year voyage on the *Beagle* gathering specimens. In 1859 he published the landmark *Origin of Species* and twelve years later in 1871 *The Descent of Man.*

The Universe. Darwin observed, especially on his *Beagle* voyage, that although organisms reproduce prolifically, at a geometric pace, there remains a kind of steady-state of numbers within a species. In this observation he was influenced and supported by the earlier work of Thomas Malthus (1766–1834). The conclusion Darwin drew was that there was a struggle for survival—which Herbert Spencer (1820–1903) would later designate "survival of the fittest"—which resulted in the continued existence of those forms most adaptable to their environment. The variations that make such success possible are transmitted to the next generation genetically, and thus nature and species evolve.

Accordingly the view of the universe as a set and finished piece, called into being at a stroke by an over-arching intelligence, was put up for challenge. At the very least, an alternate model was now available. The universe could be viewed not only as working its way toward a kind of pre-ordained destiny through timeless species and structures, but as moving blindly along with no higher value or goal than sheer survival. A middle position would emerge, of course, represented by American clergyman Lyman Abbott (1835–1922) which chose to see evolution as "God's way of doing business."

Humanity. Not all were as sanguine as the Reverend Abbott, neither in the clerical nor in the scientific realms. And many simply saw in Darwin's work the greatest shock to human dignity since the jolting of the Copernican Revolution itself. Humanity might now be seen on a continual spectrum with the rest of the animal kingdom, its dignity and destiny at discount. This conclusion was not a necessary one, we would be quick to point out, but it was at the time a plausible one.

The argument, after all, went far beyond whether one read Genesis figuratively or literally. Issues wide and deep were at stake. Frank McConnell has written in *The Science Fiction of H.G. Wells:*

In 1859, a quiet, almost pathologically shy naturalist named Charles Darwin published a book with the daunting title *On the Origin of Species by Means of Natural Selection* and the world was never the same. If Darwin was right, then mankind was demoted. No longer lord of the world, a special creation with a special mission in history, it was simply a random and temporarily successful adaption of the primal world-stuff in its ceaseless blind struggle to survive.

Darwin described an organic world of constant blind flux, struggle and variation without purpose. . . .

At a stroke, human civilization became the product of blind chance and galactic accident. Culture, purpose, consciousness, became arbitrary, momentary things. Morality becomes a temporary compromise of the life force with universal entropy.

The Flaw. Although Darwin himself was far from a radical type personally, the implications of his work could not be gainsaid. If survival in the environment was the fundamental item on the human agenda, then it is difficult not to conclude that the basic human flaw is in failure to adjust and failure to change. Stability and reverence for the past would accordingly be displaced as values in favor of adaption and experimentation. These, at least, are some of the cultural implications of the Darwinian view.

The Remedy. On the question of how to deal with the human predicament, the Darwinian movement split into two camps. On the one side were those who saw in evolution evidences of a "nature red in tooth and claw." Struggle, even violent struggle, may be a necessary part of the human equation. Many in this "social Darwinist" school saw in Darwin's research a justification in nature for unchecked competition in the social and economic order. This would serve the advantage, of course, of those who already held power, capital and resources.

On the other side were those pro-Darwinists who followed what has been called "instrumentalism." Humanity is not viewed by this group as just another animal grouping swept along on the evolutionary tides. Rather, through the evolution of the unique instruments of mind and morality, the human animal can choose to direct evolution, can make social/moral judgments about redistribution of wealth, for example. In short, the former group stressed the continuity of humanity with the animal kingdom; the latter group stressed the discontinuity. The first group might be identified as pessimistic and conservative, the second as optimistic and liberal.

The Darwinian world view, no matter which side of it one may follow, would provide a marked contrast to more traditional philosophic, theological and scientific systems in its approach to ultimate questions. For many of the thoroughgoing Darwinists, the questions of God, human dignity, and freedom moved to second and third levels of consideration. The basis for moral decision also took a decided turn away from traditional paths, since standards were often viewed to be themselves in a process of evolution.

Karl Marx (1818–1883)

A German, Karl Marx began his academic career in the study of the law, but changed to philosophy, taking a Ph.D. at the University of Jena in 1841. He was influenced by Hegel's system, but even more so by that of Ludwig Feuerbach (1804–1872), and he began to devise a consistently materialist philosophy with special reference to economic determinism. Marx joined the Communist League in 1847 and the following year wrote, with Engels, the *Communist Manifesto*. His *Das Kapital* first appeared in 1867. Marx lived most of his adult life in London after 1849, and there he is now buried.

The Universe. As already indicated, Marx builds upon the world views of Hegel and Feuerbach; this means that in the first place he perceives reality to be at root defined by motion, struggle, turmoil; it further means that it is a universe without any god,

creator or general intelligence. In short, it is a materialist universe in a dialectical process. Marx has taken Hegel's threefold thesis–antithesis–synthesis structure, stripped it of spiritual concomi-`
tants, and added to it a strong economic factor. Hence, his system often goes by the name dialectical materialism.

Humanity. Marx's view of humanity is that it is primarily materialist, determined and social. Like everything else in the universe, humanity is governed by the cosmic law of struggling material in motion. Men and women are, in fact, largely defined by the resources that are at their disposal. On one hand, Marx can be faulted here for discounting such factors as family, character, faith or will that have classically been seen as primary identity factors. But on the other hand his prevailing insight was that individuals quickly become locked in grinding, life-sapping jobs with no prospect for education, advancement, or human aspirations. Countless millions *can* in fact be set into a defined place largely shaped by lack of good nutrition, medical care, housing, clothing and education.

All this goes to say that for Marx, humanity is largely in a determined situation. The determinism is not complete, to be sure. At the end of the 1848 *Manifesto* are to be found the famous words that argue for action, and thus imply some level of freedom: "Workers of the world unite. You have nothing to lose but your chains." Still, the cards have been dealt out and not well or fairly. One of the economic-social blocks that abets this inequality will be, for Marx, organized religion. But his views on that subject we will examine in Unit Three.

Marx's view of the social dimension of human nature makes clear that Marx was not only a social critic; he was also a dreamer and a believer in great possibilities for humanity. Humanity can advance to a better relationship, even at last, Marx thought, to a classless and stateless society. There is a drive for brotherhood and sisterhood and equality somewhere deep in the Marxian vision. The embodying of that particular vision in history has been a different and often tragic story.

The Flaw. In one word, Dr. Marx's diagnosis of the trouble with his patient, humanity, was this: alienation. Men and women are not truly at home in the world; they are aliens. They are separated and cut off:

> from self-worth;
> from necessary physical resources;
> from true community.

Marx could see no escape from this crisis for the condition of unchecked capitalism in mid-nineteenth century Europe and America. He would accept no halfway remedies; in fact he thought the situation would need to get worse before it could at last change drastically for the better.

The Remedy. The prescription Marx recommended was a harsh and dreadful one: revolution in the full sense of the world. Violent revolution. The dethroning of the haves by the have-nots, the seizing of the means of production and the abolition of private property. This change in political and social structure, he believed, would be a starting point for the recasting of the human heart, for the overcoming of alienation.

As the Marxist system developed in history it came to certain conclusions: the great masses of people were so oppressed that they didn't know what was best for themselves. An elite cadre— the Party— would need to take up the banner and lead the people, even if they were in fact unwilling. The undemocratic means were to be justified by the great end of a transformed humanity.

Sigmund Freud (1856–1939)

Although Freud is regarded by many as more of a twentieth than a nineteenth century thinker, the fact remains that his most seminal work *On the Interpretation of Dreams* was researched and written at the end of the old century, being published in 1900. A Viennese psychoanalyst, Freud lived a rather quiet, ordinary life in academia and in private clinical practice. In his later years, suffering from mouth cancer, he was harassed from Vienna by the Nazis and died in London in 1939. Like Darwin and Marx before him, Freud is one of the landmarks of the modern, one of those with whom one must reckon if one is to grasp the modern consciousness and to appreciate the shaking of the foundations. The seismic shock continues into our own days.

Universe. Dr. Freud was not professionally much concerned with many of the great cosmic questions of the structure of the universe. His system is void of any God, to be sure, and we will examine his reasons for that in a later chapter. But rather than speculate about materialism, idealism or the beginning or end of time and creation, Freud chose the study of the psyche as the royal road to the heart of the truly real.

Humanity. The Freudian system is well enough known to need only the most basic review here. Humanity, according to Freud, is layered, conflictual and determined. The inner life is mysterious as well as multi-layered. The conscious mind forms but some small percentage of all that we truly are. The conscious life is much like the tip of an iceberg. Beneath the tip is something like a vast, unchartered continent made up of three regions: the id, the instinctual drives seeking immediate gratification; the ego, a kind of primitive conscience, limiting the id for the purpose of maintaining the life and health of the organism; and the superego, limiting the id for the purpose of both individual and social survival. The later Freud also spoke of the great forces of eros (life) and thanatos (death) contending within the unconscious structure of the psyche.

These inner forces are in constant turmoil, struggling one against another. In this, then, Freud is joined to Marx and Darwin in sensing reality as dynamic and tumultuous. Conflict was inevitable. The basic question would be how to cope with such conflict, how to react.

Quite early in each individual life these reactions are programmed—by parents, siblings, playmate peers, society, religion. Thus many of our most basic drives, attitudes, fears, aspirations are set for us without our knowledge or choice. There is little room for genuine freedom within such an accounting.

The Flaw. The flaw in which large segments of the race are caught is that of *repression,* a condition of poor adjustment to the inevitable conflicts of the inner self. Faced with the primal human drives for nourishment, sex, security or such great human emotions as fear, anger or love, the individual learns that these often cannot be immediately or completely gratified. What are the options?

Consider the primal emotion of anger. Suppose you work daily with an individual who becomes more unfair and abusive toward you. How to react? On one extreme there is the response of total instinctual release: you pummel the offender into insensibility. But society and personnel directors frown on this sort of thing. On the other extreme, you pretend to yourself that it isn't happening and try to ignore it all; this is repression. According to Freud, a primal emotion repressed or denied will always surface in some way, usually in some neurotic or unusual activity. A severe repression may result in the more severe fact of psychosis, a partial or complete splitting of the individual's consciousness from reality.

The middle position would be suppression. You deny the violent release, but you admit to or "own" the emotion and come to grips with it in some creative way: verbal confrontation, out-letting with a counselor or third party, physical exercise and so forth. When this suppression takes place in a sexual context, the process is usually referred to as sublimation.

Freud is best known popularly, of course, as the man who tried to break down sexual inhibitions. This is but partly true. A child of the Victorian age, Freud was well aware of the obsession with sexuality, often from a puritanical or fearful point of view that was part of the age. And many of Freud's own followers considered that he made genital sexuality far too central in his life readings. But Freud was far from the libertine that the popular imagination has made out. He was at a far remove from an "anything goes" mentality and in fact saw sexuality as needing as much contextualizing as any other human activity.

The Remedy. Not only individuals become repressed, mentally ill and dangerous, Freud thought. Societies are susceptible to the same contagion. From the social point of view, Freud could but hope for a more creative, less repressive approach to life-at-large.

For individuals, Freud pioneered his method of psychoanalysis. It could be, in the event, long, costly and painful. Beneath our surface self, Freud maintained, was the seething interior of conflict and mixed motivations and drives. To get beneath the neurotic symptoms to the conflicts causing them, Freud sought ways to probe the "heart of darkness," the inner jungle. If the conscious mind repressed the conflicts what hope had he of such discovery?

His method was to take advantage of those vulnerabilities in the blocking mechanism of the conscious life. Thus, in sleep and dreams, free-association, hypnosis and the now-famous Freudian slips, one could find the realities behind the surface of consciousness. Once the original conflicts were laid bare, the individual (with the therapist) could try to devise new and creative ways to come to grips with the real problem.

Later psychologists, pupils, and followers of Freud would differ with him in many significant ways; they would dispute over such now well-known theories as infantile sexuality or the Oedipal complex. They would replace his centrality of genital sexuality as the basic human dynamic with the drive for meaning (Frankl) or the drive for individuation integrated through the collective unconscious (Jung). All later thinkers paid tribute to Freud, however, for coming to grips with psychological conditions that relate something about the race at large, not just about a few troubled individuals.

We turn next to an examination of some major twentieth century thinkers to see how they have developed the work of these nineteenth century leaders. Finished with that examination, we will begin to search out the responses of religion to the shaking of the human foundations.

Further Reading

Clark, Ronald. *Freud: The Man and the Cause* (New York: 1980).

Fromm, Erich. *The Greatness and Limitations of Freud's Thought* (New York: 1980). Posthumously published.

Hall, Calvin. *A Primer of Freudian Psychology* (New York: 1954).

Himmelfarb, Gertude. *Darwin and the Darwinian Revolution* (Garden City: 1962).

Küng, Hans. *Freud and the Problem of God* (New Haven: 1979).

Lash, Nicholas. *A Matter of Hope: A Theologian's Reflections on the Thought of Karl Marx* (Notre Dame: 1982).

Padover, Saul. *Karl Marx: An Intimate Biography* (New York: 1978).

Stevenson, Leslie. *Seven Theories of Human Nature* (New York: 1974).

6

Redefining the Human:
Twentieth Century Examples

"Be patient toward all that is unsolved in your heart
and try to love the questions themselves."
Rainer Maria Rilke (1875–1926)

Perhaps no philosophic approach has so symbolized or marked the twentieth century as that of existentialism. Its roots have been traced to all manner of earlier thinkers: Augustine, Thomas Aquinas, Pascal, Kierkegaard. In sober truth, the existential mood is to be found in titles ranging from Kierkegaard's *Fear and Trembling* to Woody Allen's *Love and Death*. Existentialists have been a varied lot: some are highly political, others retiring; some are deeply religious, others atheistic. What are some of the insights that link together such a diversity?

Let it be first understood that before all else, existentialism is a philosophic *method* that can encompass quite varied judgments and contents. As a method, its main note is the insistence that truth is to be found not so much in ideas, ideals, abstractions or mathematical certitudes; rather, ultimate truth is to be discovered only by attention to primal inner phenomena. Often earlier philosophies wrote off such realities as the primal emotions of fear, hope, love, anxiety, insecurity as inappropriate to the philosophic task. The existentialist chose to place these at the very center of consideration.

With this understood as an opening presumption, it might then be possible (in typical oversimplified fashion) to summarize existentialist themes under three categories:

(1) Individual human beings and their primal emotions, drives and feelings are at the center of philosophic concerns, not general theories; the unique is more important than the typical.

(2) The inner, subjective experience is more revealing about reality than scientific "objective" truth; meaning and interpretation take precedence over mere facticity.

(3) More than any other, freedom is the defining human capacity; individuals, to be authentic, must choose their own interpretations, meaning and values in life.

Given these orientations in common, the existentialists derive quite different conclusions, as we have already indicated. Most basic in the division among them is that of their religious stance. One group, the non-theists, include such names as Jean-Paul Sartre, Albert Camus, and (arguably) Martin Heidegger. The theistic group would number among its members Martin Buber and Abraham Heschel (Jewish), Paul Tillich and Rudolf Bultmann (Protestant), and Gabriel Marcel and Thomas Merton (Roman Catholic).

The critical difference between the two groups comes in their interpretation of the phenomena of inner experience. The non-theists look at the basic human drives, miseries and shattered hopes and conclude that life is useless passion (Sartre) or absurdity (Camus) in the face of which the supreme act of human courage is heroic resistance. The theists examine the same phenomena and conclude differently: the very fact of the intensity and reality of our longings suggests that they are rooted in existential possibility. Our homesickness suggests not that we are orphans, but that we are hungry for a home rightly ours. As Martin Luther King expressed it: we live in the colony of time, but in the empire of eternity.

Because this unit is primarily concerned with thinkers who have tried to recast the understanding of the human in primarily non-religious terms, the first examination here will be of the thought of Jean-Paul Sartre. The approach of some of the religious existentialists will be studied in units three and four. Following the consideration of Sartre here, attention will be paid to two other writers: B. F. Skinner and Konrad Lorenz. Not existentialists as such, they are, however, decided examples of twentieth century thinkers forging a new set of answers to the fundamental human questions.

Jean-Paul Sartre (1905–1980)

A French existentialist, Sartre wrote philosophical treatises of great difficulty such as *Being and Nothingness* (1943). He was better known, though, for his use of other literary forms as in the novel *Nausea* (1939) and the play *No Exit* (1944). Sartre remained a Marxist all of his adult life. In 1964 he declined the Nobel Prize.

Universe. In Sartre's universe, there is no over-arching God, destiny or purpose. His is a postulatory atheism; he doesn't argue his way to it, but presumes the absence of God in the world or cosmos as a settled cultural fact. The universe has no meaning, except that with which human freedom invests it.

Humanity. "The hole in being" is what Sartre once called the human enterprise, in good existential fashion. Humanity is that one thing we know of on the planet that doesn't quite fit in. It is both like and unlike every other thing, especially every other animal. That which makes it unique is precisely its "innerness," or, more precisely still, its freedom. "Man is," in another famous Sartre quotation, "condemned to freedom."

We have not been created, he says, for any purpose—not by any God or evolution or life force or anything else. We simply exist. We are here and we have to decide what to make of it all. Life is "a useless passion." There is no destiny set for us anywhere. Each individual, in freedom, chooses the meaning of his or her own particular life. This freedom terrifies us, as Dostoevsky recognized in *The Brothers Karamazov*:

> You would go into the world . . . with some promise of freedom which men in their simplicity and their natural unruliness cannot even understand, which they fear and dread—for nothing had ever been more insupportable for a man and a human society than freedom.

Erich Fromm and several other psychologists have commented on this same freedom-flight phenomenon. There is a fear of genuine responsibility never far below the human surface, and that fear may account as much for authoritarianism and totalitarianisms in the world as the existence of a small number of power-mongers seeking might. It is not so much the strength of the individual taker of freedom as the willingness of the many to give it up.

Although they would differ greatly on the issue of pointlessness in the cosmos, the religious existentialists tend to agree much with Sartre on his point of freedom. They also make common cause, incidentally, against the thought of Freud and his determinism on this point. The religious thinkers, too, want to insist that a faith or life-stance that is merely "inherited" or uncritically assimilated can hardly be called authentic faith.

The Flaw. What is basically wrong with us is *inauthenticity*, or, in Sartrean French, *mauvaise foi*, bad faith. Humanity-at-large flees from freedom and gives itself over in servitude to social, political and religious systems that are all too willing to take advantage of the human dilemma.

The Remedy. Sartre is not at his strongest on practical remedies. To the illness of resisted freedom he offers the prescription that we must embrace freedom on peril of losing any semblance of human dignity. Clearly, in making this recommendation, Sartre has opted for at least one fixed value: honesty or authenticity. Yet, as Leslie Stevenson points out, this is one of the more troublesome points in Sartre's system: if self-knowledge and self-actualization are the primary values, if all things are utterly pointless, then on what basis must one opt for freedom over tyranny, for tenderness over terror?

B.F. Skinner (b. 1904)

Skinner, an American psychologist, is a leading exponent of behaviorism which defines human behavior and motivation in terms of physical reactions to external stimulation. His well-known writings include *Walden Two* (1948) and *Beyond Freedom and Dignity* (1971).

Universe. The wider world of at least the early Skinner is co-extensive with what natural science can describe. The only truth is that which science can tell us about nature. And if the world of art or religion should challenge such a proposition, the consistent behaviorist might reply that only science shows an accumulation of progress in history, whereas art and religion have largely squabbles and divergencies to show. Religion, in fact, is but another institution to manipulate human behavior. And value judgments—which many hold to be evidence of non-materiality and a wider dimension of life—are really but pressures to conform, exerted by subtle pressure groups. Moral decisions, in short, are only concealed commands.

Humanity. The only way to know human nature is through an empirical study of human behavior. What such a study tells us is that humanity is nearly totally determined to be what it is through force of *nurture* or environment. This will be directly opposed by the next writer considered, Lorenz, who stresses *nature* or our inner biological structure as the source of our determinations.

The Flaw. Because Skinner effectively weds science and

technology conceptually, he will believe at the outset that a basic purpose of science is not only to describe and measure and predict the behavior of things in the world, but to control them for the good. This will mean that his reading of the basic human flaw is that it is mal-control. Humanity is going to be controlled one way or another (most directly opposed, of course, to Sartre), so that its primary task is to resist bad control. Here, of course, are the very factors that prevent us calling Skinner's determinisms complete: the ability to *resist* and to *decide* between good and bad control would, presumably, argue for some room for maneuver.

The Remedy. Psychology, biology, and the other sciences have reached or are reaching points where they can offer techniques for the manipulation and control of human behavior. Thus, for the good of humanity, and to prevent destruction or runaway violence in society, it may be necessary to go beyond freedom and dignity to some abridgment of individual considerations.

This remedy has a certain appeal when one thinks of the hope of controlling genetic birth defects, or medically or chemically stabilizing a person afflicted with a deep-seated psychosis. But once the power is present, many commentators have asked: Who will control it? Who will make the right/wrong, healthy/unhealthy judgments? Historians are quick to point out that any presumption that governments or persons in power will consistently make right or selfless choices is hardly defensible from a reading of history. Does human "salvation" lie in yielding up many of the components that—for better or worse—have been primary identifiers of the human qualities as history has known them up to this time?

Konrad Lorenz (b. 1903)

Lorenz is an Austrian zoologist who studied at Columbia in New York and later taught at Vienna and Konigsberg (Kant's hometown). He received the Nobel Prize for physiology in 1973 and otherwise is best known for his book *On Aggression* (tr. 1966).

Universe. Moving away from reliance on metaphysical theories or too much cosmological speculation, Lorenz concentrates on the world as we can understand it through evolution. For him, evolution becomes the key to the ultimacy of the human, just as the psyche was for Freud, or the economic for Marx.

Humanity. The human inhabitants of the planet are shaped in their identities, motivations and attitudes not primarily by their environment or nurture (against Skinner, of course). It is biological nature, inner organic structure, that shapes us more than any other conceivable factor. From this point of view, it can be said that violence is innate in us. Like Freud's *id*, it must find a release, an outlet.

The Flaw. Like Freud, Lorenz discovers a basic conflict in us between our instincts implanted by evolution, and the moral restraints necessary to a civilized society. Humans have the added factors of intelligence, speech, and arsenals when it comes to expressions of violent impulse. The threat of extinction that hangs over humanity is a direct result of its most refined evolutionary gifts. Our primal flaws, then, are the intensity, range and capability of violence that we possess.

The Remedy. Surely, the situation looks hopeless at the outset. Humanity has aggression built into it, as well as the means of escalating that violent streak in a most sophisticated yet devastating manner. Can one speak of a remedy?

Lorenz maintains that a remedy is possible—not along the lines of some behaviorists, however. To screen out the root of aggression genetically, he maintains, is also to deflate the drives that lead to creativity, since there is a healthy aggressiveness at the basis of every drive to achieve.

The first ground for hope, Lorenz discovers, is in humanity's sense of fear and revulsion at its own aggressive potential for evil. Because we have the capacity to reason that has evolved along with the rest of us, we also have the ability to grasp the causes of aggression. This implies as well the ability to take rational steps to control and redirect the impulses of aggression.

Education is one answer, then, for Lorenz. Sport is another. Often neglected for serious consideration, the competitiveness of athletics is a wonderfully creative way of turning potential violence into released energies and comradeship. Humor becomes another critical release point in Lorenz's non-violent arsenal. Through wit and humor, we can see ourselves with some critical distance, learn not to take ourselves too seriously, and release pent-up frustration.

In an unusual kind of trio, then, education, sport and humor become remedies and hope-points for one of the generation's better known research scientists.

The century that has witnessed the birth of the Bomb, the holocaust, major wars and famines has also seen space exploration, technologies that serve human needs, and in many places expanded consciousness and exercise of civil and human rights. Perhaps in some fashion Dickens' words about the period of the French Revolution from *A Tale of Two Cities* (1859)—the best of times, the worst of times—are true of all times.

And yet, few would deny to this twentieth century of the common era uniqueness in the annals of turmoil, promise and endangerment. It would be the worst state of all if there were not serious and thoughtful thinkers trying to make sense of it all. The very attempt and search itself is a lesson in human resiliency, determination and endurance. Having looked at only a few among many contemporary attempts at coming to grips with ultimacies, we turn next to experiences of religion, past as well as present, to see what light they might shed on the baffle business.

Further Reading

Barrett, William. *Irrational Man: A Study in Existential Philosophy* (Garden City: 1962).

Beauvoir, Simone de. *Adieux: A Farewell to Sartre* (New York: 1984).

Boulding, Kenneth. *The Meaning of the Twentieth Century: The Great Transition* (New York: 1964).

Collins, James. *The Existentialists: A Critical Study* (Chicago: 1952).

Harrington, Michael. *The Politics at God's Funeral* (New York: 1983). A discussion of the grounds of modern unbelief by a former religious believer.

Küng, Hans. *On Being a Christian* (Garden City, N.Y.: 1976). A book that examines many of the reasons for unbelief and ends in religious affirmation.

Macquarrie, John. *Existentialism* (Philadelphia: 1972).

Skinner, B.F. *Particulars of My Life* (New York: 1975).

Unit Three:

Religious Responses

7

Defining Religion

"For the secret of man's being is not only to live, but
to have something to live for."
Fyodor Dostoevsky (1821–1881)

Incredible as it may seem, social scientists can agree fairly readily on this statement: All societies have had religion in one
form or another. At a time when it is difficult to find professional
agreements in many areas, that bare statement of itself may be
something of an accomplishment. As to what religion actually
means, or where it came from, or what are its primary functions,
on these issues the wrangling begins.

Religion has been variously described, in both positive and
negative ways. Marx considered it a human invention to deflect
consideration of economic and social suffering. Freud similarly
read religion as a human construct to screen us from harsh psychological realities. Emile Durkheim (1858–1917), a French sociologist, concluded that religion is primarily a communal reality,
and is in fact the product of society's own powers and drives. It
is like society itself divinized and projected into rites, totems and
divinities. William James (1842–1910), a pioneer American psychologist, stressed instead the individuality of religion as psych-
ically organizing and regenerating.

And if there is an assembly of thinkers to suggest that religion
is primarily a human *projection*, the product of a fear-inspired belief in dreams, spirits in nature and the unknown, another group
of thinkers from Augustine (354–430) to Protestant theologian
Karl Barth (1886–1968) want to stress religion as human *recep-*

tion of a divine revelation. Religious philosophers and theologians of the western world have generally tended to blend these realities, speaking of religion as a result of the *action* of God and the free *reaction* of the human.

This chapter intends to make modest ventures into this definitional jungle in the following manner:

(1) A review of definitions of religion from several sources.
(2) A study of basic types of religion.
(3) A presentation of selected criteria for genuine religion.

The chapter that follows will likewise take up a threefold task.

(1) An examination of constants in the history of religion.
(2) An analysis of the human and religious act of faith.
(3) A presentation of distinctive themes from some of the major world religions.

Definitions of Religion from Several Sources

The first two definitions to be examined are negative and have been especially influential in the last century. The remaining ones to be considered are appreciative of religion. All of these definitions approach religion from a *functional* point of view. They address the usefulness (or lack of it) of religion to individuals and societies without concentrating on the hard question of the truth or falsity of religion as such. That investigation, to some extent, is the burden of the last unit of this study.

1. Religion as Social Pacifier

Karl Marx, as described earlier, saw the world in terms of the conflict of the economically powerful and the economically powerless. From that point of view, he considered religion as a major power working to maintain the unjust status quo. This it accomplished by turning the minds of its adherents to an afterlife of supposed redress of injustices. But the path to that heavenly utopia was along passive acceptance of things as they are. The other-worldly interests of Judaism and Christianity in particular for Marx, then, were to turn attention and action away from this world. Thus, he formulated his famous claim that religion was "the sigh of the oppressed creature" and "the opium of the people," drugging them from the full force of reality.

Marx further judged that as the population-at-large began to acquire the good things of the earth (through revolution), the need for religion would diminish, and the reality itself would eventually wither away. Yet, whereas many atheists of the eighteenth century took a kind of tolerant disdain for religion, thinking of it as a kind of sop for the masses until enlightenment swept it away (Voltaire, of course was something of an exception), Marx was more aggressively anti-religious, always seeing religion as a counter-revolutionary force that would need help in disappearing.

How did religious scholars react to Marx? Primarily in two ways:

(1) They agreed that religion had, in fact, often been used as a retrogressive force in society. But a good thing, the argumentation went on, could be badly used. Religion needn't be a turning from the present, but often represented both a force for enhancing of human life and social justice.

(2) They pointed out, especially in the twentieth century situation in the industrialized countries, that as workers gained more affluence, their religious needs did not wither, but, in a sense, could be said to have increased. Relieved from the sheer struggle for survival and basic needs, they began to seek out a meaning for the human enterprise in a more fundamental sense.

2. *Religion as Psychological Projection*

Sigmund Freud also was an active opponent of the traditional religious perspective. His short 1927 work on religion indicates by its title alone his feeling: *The Future of An Illusion*. Religion, Freud considered, is a human construct, a psychological projection of the lost father figure. We invent a father-god in order to feel more secure and at home in an alien, indifferent, even hostile universe. But this represents repression, a failing to come to grips with reality and thus presents a fertile ground for the growth of neurosis and psychosis. If humanity is to become more healthy psychologically, religion had to go.

To be sure, as we have already seen, many of Freud's own psychological followers came up with more positive approaches to religion. But again, we ask, what were the responses of thoughtful theologians in the wake of Freud's very serious theological challenge?

(1) They pointed out that the God of the western religions—Judaism, Christianity, Islam—provided not just comfort in the lives of believers, but challenge and *in*security. Nowhere was this more apparent than in the fulminations of the Hebrew prophets.

(2) They pointed out that Freud's own argument had an assumption lurking beneath it: that *because* humanity longs desperately for something or someone, thereby it *must* be non-existent. And where, they asked, was the scientific warrant for that position? They thus inverted Freud's own analysis to suggest (as Jung did in part) that a drive so profoundly rooted in the human psyche could well point to a cosmic reality printed into the psychic structure, but existing beyond it as well.

(3) They noted that Freud's fear of human projection was not far distant from the western religion's own terror—enshrined in

the *first* commandment—that humans are idol-making creatures, always tempted to project a god in their own image.

The presentation of these theological rejoinders to Marx and Freud, let it be quickly noted, are not placed here as facile responses or "put-downs." More than anything, they are meant to suggest that religious scholarship, while not caving in before the thought of these critics, had to admit that even from their own point of view, the attacks were partially well-aimed. The religions had been caught in a vulnerable position, and part of twentieth century theology has been a reflection of their own reformulations in the light of such critiques.

3. Religion as Reaching for the Eternal

The first positive description of religion that we examine comes from a quite ancient and venerable source, Plato (427–347 B.C.). It was the twentieth century philosopher of science Alfred Whitehead (1861–1947) who commented that all philosophy has been a footnote to Plato. He meant, of course, that Plato set up for the western world our very way of formulating philosophical questions.

Plato's own view of religion may have been somewhat limited by his respect for the anthropomorphic gods of Olympus for which the Greeks were famous. To what extent he accepted their actual existence has been a lively subject of historical debate. But it is Plato's general philosophical religious perspective that we wish to indicate here.

Following a line of earlier thinkers himself, Plato became nonetheless the first massively influential Greek writer to argue that things are not merely what they seem to be. There is a depth, a dimensionality to reality that is not immediately evident to the senses. This world of *ideas* or *ideals* or *forms* is the ultimately real—more real, in fact, than the physical world that we sense around us on every side. What's more, this ideal world is eternal, changeless, lasting.

At first hearing, Plato's thought sounds, literally, incredible. But how could Plato have become "the father of western thought" if his basic point of view was so seemingly wildly imaginary? This calls for some examining.

When Plato looked around him (when we look around ourselves)—what did he see (what do we see?) He saw men, women, trees, grass, buildings, roads, food, cups. At any given time, if asked this question, we might answer that we see about ten or twenty or fifty things around us. But look closer, Plato would urge. In a way you are seeing thousands and thousands of things: blades of grass, fingers on people and feathers on chickens. We do not just see a million things when we look about. We see *types* of things—not two million unrelated atoms—but repeatable, predictable sorts of beings.

A Greek thinker a generation older than Plato, Democritus (460–370 B.C.), had already propounded the theory that reality is made up merely of material atoms in motion in the void. Plato distanced himself radically from this mechanistic viewpoint. In place of pointless *chaos,* he wished to stress *cosmos,* harmony, pattern, order, repeatability.

Plato then argued that behind the individual things that we see there are forms that make them to be what they are: treeness, chairness, humanness. If this sounds odd, he would argue, consider the alternative: the types we see are but accidents, not interrelated at all, simply happenings.

A contemporary example may bring Plato's thought into some focus. Imagine yourself waiting in line for an interminable time to buy tickets for a film, a rock concert or a Derby pari-mutuel bet. Suddenly a large individual walks up, breaks the line and goes to its head. The crowd is enraged. Why? The individual has broken no law that is to be discovered on the books in any county or state.

This bold, brash individual has violated a *principle*—that of fair play. Translated in this instance, it means that we all wait our turn in line. It is a *non-physical* idea, if you will, that has physical consequences—in this case, perhaps a brawl—a fact of the senses flowing from that which is not itself sensible, but a principle. This example, weak as it may be, reflects in some sort Plato's belief in a non-physical world surrounding and *grounding* our physical one.

If forms exist, they are unseen, but profoundly real. In fact, individual manifestations of the form will come to be and pass away (*this* tree, *this* man, *this* woman), but tree, man, woman, continue. Accordingly, the world of forms is primal; it comes before and makes all the rest possible. It is timeless, eternal, and structured. Furthermore, it is hierarchical. That is to say, some forms are higher, some lower than others. The highest forms are the Good, the True and the Beautiful.

Plato's confidence in certitude, in knowability, in a pattern to be found in nature and humanity and cosmos quite simply made western science and education possible. There is no way to overstate the importance of Plato to western philosophy and religion. His longing for the eternal, for the Highest Forms, would mark the religion of the west ever after. His confidence that reality extends beyond the senses alone is a bedrock of western understanding. It haunts modern thought, even when its opponents strive mightily to oppose it.

Perhaps Plato's most dramatic telling of his vision of reality is in the famous cave sequence at the end of the *Republic*. Imagine, he says, a cave in which some men have long been chained. They sit so that they face a wall; and on this wall they see shadows and images cast by figures walking about outside, the shadows being made through the light from a fire outside. Suppose further, Plato now says, that one of the prisoners gets the notion to break away and explore things a bit. He escapes and goes outside the cave only to discover an immensely vaster world of three dimensions, color and intensity. He returns to the cave, eager to "liberate" his companions and awaken them to this exciting, wider world. They, in their fear and love of mediocrity and shadows, choose to stay where they are.

The shadow world represents the world as we know it by the senses alone. The real world (of forms) is not divorced from the senses, but expands and fulfills them. Still, Plato suggests, those who bring such truth will always have to pay a terrible price. His own teacher, Socrates, of course, had been executed in the line of truth-telling.

4. Religion as Value Definer

Psychologist Erich Fromm wrote in *Psychoanalysis and Religion:* Religion is "any system of thought or action shared by a group which gives the individual a frame of orientation and an object of devotion." Religion from this point of view is seen as guarding a life against formlessness and purposelessness. Religion is that symbol system, perception of reality, or insight into the reality of things (God, if one chooses) that provides the individual with a destiny, a direction, and a dignity.

From the very etymology of the word, *re-ligio,* religion has traditionally been taken to mean a linking back, a bridging of a being into a context wider and deeper than the isolated self. Religion is thus seen to provide a valid ground for worship, revering and reaching beyond the self for the Source of being (perhaps with the aid of that Source). Dostoevsky wrote in *The Brothers Karamazov:* "So long as man remains free he strives for nothing so incessantly and so painfully as to find someone to worship." And Peter Shaffer has the psychologist Dysart say in his very important play *Equus:* "Without worship, you shrink; it's as brutal as that."

The need for worship, for a fitting object of human love and adoration, is hardly a recent discovery. Augustine in *The City of God* made the astute psychological observation that people are going to love, almost by nature. It is right that they do so. The core problem or flaw with us, Augustine says, is that we misplace our loves, and love too intensely the wrong things. Since we are going to be lovers anyway, we had better decide carefully whom or what we will love *because we will ultimately become like what we love.*

Religion, then, in this understanding, has to do with sorting out our priorities and loves and adorations. It helps us judge, on the basis of revelation or experience, or the evidence of a community in history, what is truly worthy of human regard and effort.

5. Religion as Evoking Reverence for Individual Life

William James, who wrote the American psychological classic *The Varieties of Religious Experience* in 1902, believed firmly that religion helps the individual attain a profound sense of self-worth, both in the eyes of the deity and of the self. This is perceived as a starting point for all other regard and achievement. Healthy religion, then (and James is quite willing to admit that it can take on sick manifestations as well), results in a gathering of scattered energies, and an intensified feeling for life and its possibilities. Religion is thus the ally of psychological wholeness and human development.

An earlier American thinker, Henry David Thoreau (1817–1862), by no means a traditional or orthodox believer, yet revealed in *Walden Pond* something of a religious orientation to life in his drive to reverence the sacredness of the moment and the possibilities of life. When he went off to Walden Pond to live, his purpose, he said, was simple:

> I went to the woods because I wished to live deliberately, to front only the essential facts of life, and see if I could learn what it had to teach, and not, when I came to die, to discover that I had not lived.

Abraham Heschel, the American Jewish writer cited in an earlier chapter, also reveals this approach to life. We take living for granted, being so busy with survival and success that we fail to appreciate the marvel of living itself. T.S. Eliot (1888–1965), the American-British poet, deplored the same human affliction in his *Love Song of J. Alfred Prufrock* (1917): "I have measured out my life with coffee spoons."

Both Eliot and Heschel, in fact, found in religion a powerful force for reawakening a sense of awe, wonder and reverence. Prayer is then seen in part as the fertile ground in which such an awakening and reverence can grow.

6. Religion as Enhancing Community and Human Relationships

A profound sense of the mystery of life, many traditional religious thinkers insist, not only leads to a heightened sense of the individual; it has a crucial impact on society as well. Martin Buber (1878–1965), the Jewish author of the famous *I and Thou* (1923), stresses the nature of life as relational ("to be is to be in relation") and the role of religion as constantly urging us to make of relationality all that it should be.

We are, in large part, defined by our relationships—with our own better self, with others we know, with society-at-large, and with God. To live is to live in a web of relationships and interconnectedness. It is the thought of John Donne revisited: "No man is an island," entire unto himself. From this point of view, religion could never be seen as Whitehead once described it as what people do with their "solitariness." Rather, it is what people do to enhance and make real the grace of their relatedness.

Among other religious figures who saw religion primarily in terms of a commitment to community and its development and improvement (again sometimes at the price of resistance and suffering) are:

Albert Schweitzer (1875–1965), Alsatian scholar and theologian, acquired four doctorates in various academic areas and went off to spend his life as a medical missionary in Gabon.

Mohandas Gandhi (1869–1948) combined mysticism with political action in bringing independence to India.

Martin Luther King (1929–1968) developed a non-violent civil rights revolution in the United States after a study of the Protestant Social Gospel tradition and the thought of Gandhi.

One more religious thinker whose special stress was on religion as opening humanity to the depths of reality of the person and community as grounded in the call and grace of God was French Jesuit scientist Pierre Teilhard de Chardin (1881–1955). Teilhard developed a complex view of the universe in which cosmic evolution is seen as directional rather than haphazard or accidental. God is seen as Alpha and Omega, beginning and end, drawing life forth to ever higher forms of complexity and consciousness so that it might respond in freedom to the divine summons. Teilhard's much disputed vision emphasizes that cosmic evolution itself is oriented to person and interrelatedness; these become supreme values in his world view.

7. Religion as Developer of Quality Life Responses

All lives eventually get around to times of loneliness, sorrow, suffering and unhappiness. If these are inevitabilities, then the crucial question is how each individual shall respond to them. In fact, the case has been made over and again that we are defined not so much by the "givens" of our lives over which we have no control as by the response we make to the things that are. It was John Lennon who sagely observed that life is what happens to us while we are busy making other plans.

One of religion's historical roles has been in helping individuals develop a quality response to loneliness, to pain, to suffering and to death itself. Rather than cynicism or bitterness, the religions have fostered attitudes that help people to integrate the negative and positive sides of their experience. Swiss Catholic writer Hans Küng states in *On Being a Christian* (1976):

> (Christians) can support a truly radical humanism which is able to integrate and cope with what is untrue, not good, unlovely, inhuman not only everything positive, but also . . . everything negative, even suffering, sin, death and futility.

Basic Types of Religion

Through all the varying emphases, it is possible to discern certain aspects of the definition of religion by the thinkers we have examined. Without locking writer or reader into a definition as such, it is possible to list these awarenesses:

1. That there is more to reality than that which is immediately sense perceivable.

2. That this something more is in fact a spiritual or transcendent dimension of existence that exists within and around our "ordinary" experience, but is not co-extensive with it.

3. That this transcendence is the ground or source of being, a God who may or may not be perceived as personal, but who is perceived as benevolent toward created things.

4. That this Ground of Being has profound impact and implications in shaping the self-worth, moral life and reach for excellence of individuals and societies.

5. That in both life's positive and negative experiences, there is meaning, pattern, endurance to be perceived and achieved through both prayer and moral action.

6. That through such experiences and actions, individuals can be linked or related to their Source, their better selves, their own community as well as the vaster community of the earth, living, dead, and yet to be.

Within the world of religion, as we have already discerned, there is wide variation and point of view. In fact, John Edward Sullivan in *The Great Ideas Today: 1977* has drawn on an immense amount of religious phenomenological study to produce the following listing of five basic kinds of religion. They represent, of course, not necessarily opposed types, but differing emphases, ripe for interrelating. In each case, type is listed first by its object, followed by the typical human response to that object. Also noted with each pairing are leading representatives of the type:

Ceremonial Religion: The object of the religious relationship is a number of suprahuman, personal beings who are freely active in a beneficial way.

Religious activity consists of actions and words that express real and continuing dependence on the beneficent activity of suprahuman personal beings.

Representatives: Plato and Cicero

Moral Religion:

The object of the religious relationship is an entity of the highest moral character that is not active in any way in human affairs.

Religious activity consists of the exercise of the socio-moral virtues in imitation of, or in confrontation with, the ultimate moral being.

Representatives: Rousseau and Kant

Mystical Religion:

The object of the religious relationship is the one and only really real, which is not finally distinct from the best in human beings.

Religious activity consists of an inner quest for realization of unification with the one profoundly real that entails a process of disengagement from otherness and individuality.

Representatives: Plotinus and Sankara

Revealed Religion:

The religious object is the revealing God, the one and only supreme Creator, a personal being of moral excellence who is freely active in human affairs in a beneficial way, and who has intervened definitively in human history to reveal himself and to establish a visible community as the bearer of the true religion.

Religious activity consists of a complex, divinely aided human response to a unique divine initiative; the elements of this response are faith in the revealing God and obedience to divine commands that require ceremonial activities, socio-moral living, and the love of God and man.

Representatives: Philo, Augustine and Al Ghazali

Secular Religion: The religious object is an intrahistorical idealized humanity which lies within the active powers and capacities of mankind.

Religious activity consists of all human activity that effectively and consciously cooperates in the realization of idealized humanity in history.

Representatives: Comte and Feuerbach

Criteria for Genuine Religion

In the welter of so many types of religion, is it possible to establish any criteria for true/false or healthy/unhealthy religions? What is one to do, for instance, if an individual claims to have a direct revelation from God that all blue-eyed people are superior to all brown-eyed people and are to be treated as such? Are we absolutely vulnerable to having to admit any subjective and privatized report as religious, even if it is experienced with great intensity? A Hitler, after all, felt very intensely about his perceptions of life; yet the consequences are well enough known not to need detailing.

Joachim Wach, a pioneering professor in the history of religion at the University of Chicago, addressed this difficult question after the most thorough study of the history of religions. His result was a listing of four criteria for genuine as opposed to bogus religious experience. The listing may be quite basic and minimal, yet it is a safety shield culled from the histories of the great religions to ward off psychosis trying to pass for religion.

Thus, Wach argues in *Types of Religious Experience* that valid religious faith involves ultimacy, totality, intensity and community. From his researches, religion:

1. Is a response to what is experienced as *ultimate* reality. It cannot end up in the worship of the trivial, and it must be a *response* so that it is not totally a passive experience.

2. Involves the *total* person, not just one aspect such as mind or will or emotion; this means that being religious does not remove the obligation of the individual to think critically, to choose wisely and to experience widely and well.

3. Is at least occasionally *intense;* it is not simply another category of practical living but involves one's confrontation with the matters of life and death, meaning and purpose.

4. Issues in *action* or concern for action in the *community.* Again we find the insistence that genuine religion can never be merely an isolated, privatized experience, nor the excuse for selfishness. Rather, its basic thrust is to reach out beyond the self to others and community. The monastic traditions too of east and west are keenly aware of this fact and work to keep alive a compassionate sense of the wider world.

Further Reading

Bettis, Joseph D. (ed.) *Phenomenology of Religion: Eight Modern Descriptions of the Essence of Religion* (New York: 1969).

Noss, David S. and John B. *Man's Religions* 7th ed. (New York: 1984).

Oates, Wayne. *The Psychology of Religion* (Waco: 1973).

Ramsey, Ian. "Philosophy of Religion" in *Encyclopedia Britannica* (1974), vol. 15, pp. 592–603.

Smart, Ninian. *The Religious Experience of Mankind* 2nd ed. (New York: 1976).

Wach, Joachim. *Types of Religious Experience* (Chicago: 1965).

8

Themes of the World Faiths

"Faith keeps many doubts in her pay.
If I could not doubt, I should not believe."
Henry David Thoreau (1817–1862)

Constants in the World Religions

All religions can be classified as either *natural* (sometimes called primitive) or *historical*. Natural religions existed both in ages past as well as in many non-industrialized areas today. Millions of the planet's peoples are at this time among the followers of natural religion. Its leading characteristic is that it sees the primary avenue of humanity to the divine and of the divine back to the human through the cycles of nature. These include life-cycles of individuals (birth, growth, puberty, marriage, reproduction, death) as well as the cycles of the seasons.

The historical religions also tap into the seasonal cycles (Passover, Easter, Ramadan) and those of personal life as well (circumcision, baptism, sacraments in general). But the historical religions, while seeing the reach of God in the cycles, maintain that the divine revelation primarily comes through manifestations of God in history (Moses and the exodus, Buddha, Jesus, Muhammad).

The historical religions themselves are in turn generally subdivided into two larger groups. The eastern stem includes Hinduism, the oldest of the world's historical religions, going back to the second millennium B.C. in India, and Buddhism, derived from Hinduism in the sixth century B.C. Also in the eastern group are the religions of China, especially Confucianism and Taoism, both gaining strength about the third century B.C. On the western

90

stem are Judaism, from the middle of the second millennium B.C., Christianity, coming forth from its Jewish matrix in the first century of the common era, and Islam, finding roots in both the Old Testament, the New Testament, and most fully in the Koran, and emerging in Arabia in the seventh century as reckoned by Christianity.

All these religions—natural as well as historical—have certain factors in common. These constants, which are structural elements that might be found in other organizations and movements as well, nonetheless provide a common focus for consideration of the world's faiths. They are:

(1) *Creed*	A basic angle of vision, a way of perceiving reality. It may or may not take articulate form as in the creeds of Christianity.
(2) *Code*	A way of action or code follows upon the way one reads people or life or purpose. Some religions have a very precise code of do's and dont's; others offer more general principles and guidelines. All faiths, however, insist that a genuine faith implies moral behavior.
(3) *Ceremony*	All organized religions have ritual or worship activity in common. These help to solidify, intensify and embody the beliefs and behavioral demands of the religions. Without such ritual, the religions are convinced, human life would lose a centering and shaping force.

(4) *Community*   To keep alive religious belief and work, to
                     prevent the drift into withering isolation and
                     small-mindedness, the faiths draw their ad-
                     herents into communities and bid them be re-
                     sponsible for the wider world.

In addition, all the religions make reference to the Holy, to
Sacred Time and Space, and to the importance of Myth. Each of
these we now examine briefly in turn.

The Holy. Rudolph Otto published in 1923 a landmark book
in religious studies: *The Idea of the Holy.* In it he summed up an
experience common to all the religions, an experience that is not
reducible to psychological or philosophical or sociological analysis alone. It is *sui generis,* a unique human experience. William
James had pointed to it in his *Varieties of Religious Experience* as
well.

The Holy is the experience of the numinous, the Other, the
overwhelming and to some extent indescribable Ground of Being.
The Holy invariably triggers a twin reaction in the human family.
Humanity feels awe, fear, and distance in the face of the Holy.
But it also experiences attraction, familiarity and an openness of
the self toward the Other. For the western religions, this is sum-
marized in the call of Isaiah in the sixth chapter of the book of that
name in the Bible. Called by God, Isaiah responds: ''Holy, holy,
holy, Lord God of Hosts,'' suggesting his distance from the Lord
as creature in the presence of Creator. But Isaiah immediately
adds: ''Heaven and earth are full of your glory''—indicating
God's presence in a familiar and constant way.

Sacred Time and Space. Another famous researcher in the
area of world religions is Mircea Eliade, still situated at the University of Chicago. In such works as *Cosmos and History* and *The
Sacred and the Profane,* Eliade relates the constancy in all religions of times and places that are set apart as special, privileged,

sacred. This establishing as sacred of certain "zones," of course, doesn't diminish other times and places to the realm of the insignificant or trivial; quite the opposite, it ennobles them by giving them a center and a significance.

The primitive religions often employ a mountain as the sacred place, a kind of visible link between earth and sky. The *axis mundi* or world's center is a visible, tangible link with power, pattern, and significance. In the historical religions, the symbolization is also crucial. Moses makes the covenant with God on Mount Sinai and Jesus makes his most pivotal pronouncement of the beatitudes (in Matthew's account) in the Sermon on the Mount.

Times too take on a specially charged importance. In the natural religions, rites of passage dramatically reflect a reaching for the moment of cosmic creativity, timelessness, limitless energy. Muslims commemorate the time of the hegira of Muhammad, Jews the time of the Passover, Christians the resurrection of Jesus. All of these are times that make all other time take on meaning and hope.

Even in a more secularized culture, time is never only chronology or "tick-tock" time. Greek, in fact, distinguishes *chronos,* clock-time, from *kairos,* the dramatic eruption of "the fullness of time," the highly charged and deeply personal moment. Individuals keep birthdays and anniversaries as passably "sacred" or at least special. The nation observes Independence Day and Thanksgiving as kinds of national "holy days." Places like the Statue of Liberty, Independence Hall, and the Lincoln Memorial carry much more signification weight, generation after generation, than other places like a K-Mart or a McDonalds. Time is not just time. Space is not just space. Phenomenologically, observably, in a quite real world of significances, there are differences.

Myth. Myth is not a bad word. It does not mean in the realm of religion, as it does at times in popular usage, a lie or fabrication or error. A myth is a story that may or may not have a reportorial-historical basis; it may also be an elaboration of an event that does have such an historical starting point.

The myth is a story that tells us something primal and fundamental about the human experience and condition. It often deals in archetypes or symbols, investing flesh and blood individuals with the telling of a story that is true for humanity-at-large.

Myths are powerful because they are definitional; they define and describe the reality that often lurks beneath surface appearances. Myths take on vast economic implications, as when advertising tells us, subtly or overtly, what we should eat or drive, how we should dress or smell, what, in fact, all the beautiful people in our advertising are doing. Myths have political power and consequences as well. How we image ourselves *to* ourselves as a people may well determine the electional decisions we make.

Myths, in short, open us to the underlying patterns or truths about life. Such patterns become evident in fairy tales, ballads, literature, the great Greek or Norse myths or those of other nationalities. They are also part of the private story that each of us tells to ourselves about ourselves. Joseph Campell writes in *The Masks of God: Primitive Mythology:*

> Clearly mythology is no toy for children. Nor is it a matter of merely scholarly concern, of no moment to modern men of action. For symbols . . . teach and release the deepest centers of motivation, moving literate and illiterate alike, moving mobs, moving civilizations.

The pre-eminent Carl Jung took up the subject at length in *Man and His Symbols:*

> Some symbols point to man's need for liberation from any state of being that is too immature, too fixed or final. In other words, they concern man's release from, or transcendence of,

any confining pattern of existence, as he moves toward a superior or more mature stage in his development.

Finally, the power of myth is seen here from the point of view of a Christian theologian, James P. Mackey, in ''The Faith of the Historical Jesus'' in *Horizons* (Fall 1976):

> Myth is man's attempt to give expression to his deepest and most comprehensive understanding of his condition in the universe, and to do this by the use of the richness of symbol rather than the more restrictive clarity of concepts. The symbols he uses he usually creates from those aspects of reality or experience which are most crucial for his survival.

> Revelation is the myth within all myth. That is to say, it is less a distinctive myth in its own right . . . and more the master myth that is operative in all individual myths, like the master key to a room in a building, each of which has its own individual key.

The Human Act of Faith

The underlying and sustaining dynamic of all the religions is the act of *faith,* the staking of life and the casting of meaning on that which is partially seen, partially unseen. Since faith deals with the unseen as well as the seen, since it involves an interpretive approach to reality, it is of the very lifeblood of the religious experience.

But faith is not only a religious response. It is endemic to the human structure. It is, in a sense, an ''ordinary'' human act. From this point of view, we might speak of *common* faith and *personal* faith. Common faith bespeaks the most ordinary way in which we live our lives. We can't be certain that other drivers will stop at red lights, or that traffic signals will function aright, or that the chef in the college cafeteria hasn't poisoned everyone intentionally on a particularly bad day. But we live our days with the common faith that these dire things will not happen. We act as if they will not. We act in a common faith. Not to act, to wait for utter certitude, would be to experience a kind of fearful frozenness rather than life.

Personal faith moves to a deeper level of the psychological and emotional life. All people feel the need to trust and be trusted by at least a few special people. To find that a close friend has betrayed us is not on the same par emotionally with the news that our tire is flat. When we allow others to become close friends, we in effect invite them to shape our lives, our feelings, our emotions, our self-perceptions. This, in fact, is why close friendship is both a gift and a vulnerability. The kind of faith that we invest in others and ask others to bestow upon us is yet another example of the way in which faith is endemic or basic to the human structure, even before it becomes a religious act.

Additionally, faith can be said to be not only endemic, but interpretive and integrating as well. That is to say, faith on the human level represents that way of reading reality that we have discussed before. And not only do we think about reality, but we must act on it as well, again without full certitude of results. How are we to integrate the various levels of our lives: emotional, moral, intellectual? How do we know which profession to pursue? How should we proceed in a friendship? Whom can we trust? All these questions deal in the need for integration of action in our lives, and all of them also invite that very action in the absence of assurances of result: that is to say, risk; that is to say, faith.

Even before the religious equation enters, then, faith is a profoundly human act. But with the consideration of the divinity as a partner to the act of believing, the stakes become higher, more ultimate, and, from a certain point of view as well, more human.

To speak of religious faith in this way, it needs to be remembered, is to speak of faith as an experience of trust involving a person's totality. We speak not just of mental assent to propositions on the one extreme, or to deeply felt warmth devoid of intellectual and critical depth on the other. Faith relates, as Protestant theologian Paul Tillich wrote, to the ultimate questions that our life's experience bring before us. Faith is at every point connected to the turmoil and even the mess of living; it is not a retreat or an escape from it.

Faith, according to the major nineteenth century Catholic thinker John Henry Cardinal Newman (1801–1890), might be called from one point of view a convergence of probabilities. It may be that reason can bring us part of the way that religious insight travels. But reason alone can never prove all the dimensions of the living God as God is described in the great religions of the west.

Rather, our experience of life orients us in a certain direction to accept coherence and purpose in the universe-at-large as well as in our personal lives. But life also brings us negative data—suffering children and holocausts and thousands of other horrors—that can lead us to question and even to turn aside from the religious sensibility. The probabilities of life at last, for Newman, converge to make faith not unreasonable or untenable; they lead to an openness, to a revelational reading of the pattern of things that does not deny conscience or intelligence. But we have only a convergence—more probability than certitude, in a subjective sense. How are we to react?

The primal religious act of faith for Newman would be then to choose the unknown and the possible in the light of the partially known. We make an act of faith and risk whereby we opt not only for or against God or Christianity or faith, but in important ways for a self-definition as well.

Here we are in confrontation with one of those great questions we approached in the beginning of our study. If the facts of faith are really so critical, why are they not obvious to all people readily? Why must they be thought through and lived through so painfully? Why all the risk and unclarity?

Newman's instinct for response is very important. His sensibilities lead us to conclude that for him the most critical factors in our lives are precisely those with the least certitudes about them: love, friendship, career, life philosophy. There is a direct proportion between the preciousness of these elements of our lives, and the amount of struggle and self-investment it took to make them really and fully our own.

Here we find existential themes of freedom rising once again. Our great task in life is to become a true self. And that means risk, loss, pain; but it also means authentic self-possession and a partnership with the divine creativity. The individual struggles in the darkness because he or she has seen particles of light; the further life-work, then, after these moments of grace or insight is to set about making that light reflective of the true, inner, unique self.

This emphasis is at the heart of the work of Soren Kierkegaard who has already been mentioned. Standing in the tradition himself of a man like Pascal who saw humanity cast somewhere between greatness and insignificance, Kierkegaard spoke of human fragility and insecurity as a decided asset to authentically achieved humanity.

In a closely reasoned and famous text called *Stages on Life's Way* (1846), Kierkegaard argued for three stages of human growth; these are not necessarily progressive. One individual may find all of them inside the self at one given time. First is the *aesthetic* stage at which the most important thing in life for the individual is the immediate gratification of sensual and bodily needs. This, Kierkegaard need hardly insist, is worthy and important enough as far as it goes. But the point is, precisely, how far does it go? As the ultimate reason for human existence, not far. Don Juan became Kierkegaard's model here as one who had more and more sensual experiences while finding less and less satisfaction. First came some fun, then some levels of boredom, then the nagging sense that there must be more to it all than this. At last, something akin to despair and a sense of helplessness and hopelessness sets in.

But this very despair can become the human ally. For it forces the individual to seek alternatives to the aesthetic as the final meaning of life. The next stage to be discovered in this way is the *ethical*. Now the individual, still keeping a care for the body and its needs, begins to find greater causes for which to live, and for which the body may have to sacrifice, even to die (as in a war to defend a national cause). The ethical stage suggests that standing for right against wrong, or for one's family or faith or nation, or for personal integrity—any of these must be more crucial than mere creature comfort. They point to the existence of a higher order of reality, another dimension. But still there remains a nagging incompletion. We never live up to all our high moral ideals. Grounds appear again for the despair process.

Is there perhaps a third level, then, in which humanity does not try to impose its meanings, but opens itself in faith and trust and risk to the promptings of the Spirit, of the future, of God—a level in which the intellect and will, while not disappearing, recede into the background as does also the extremely active approach to life? Here then is the famous Kierkegaardian "leap of faith." If reason made the jump for us, it wouldn't be faith. That which is cheaply gotten is cheaply held. If all things were obvious, especially the most important things, they wouldn't be precious and they wouldn't be our own.

Part and parcel of this understanding, of course, is the reality of doubt, or, perhaps better put, radical questioning. From the existential point of view, radical questioning is the shadow that proves that the substance is real in the first place. A faith that is fearful of examination is a weak and faithless faith from the start. The stronger faith, these thinkers write, is that which admits difficulties and lives with them and never ceases their exploration.

Within this general existential tradition of faith, one finds contemporary Canadian Catholic theologian Gregory Baum. There are, Baum argues in *Faith and Doctrine,* certain depth areas and questions in every life, such as the Holy, friendship, encounter, conscience, truth, solidarity, compassionate protest, rage at evil, sin and death. If faith is authentic in a life, Baum then argues, it will help to explain, enlarge and enhance these realities or our better responses to them in our lives. If this process is not occurring in our depth areas, then, Baum insists, either one's choice of religious traditions is incorrect, or (more likely) one is not attuned to all the possibilities of one's own tradition.

Themes from Eastern Religions

The search for the depths of humanity as well as divinity is to be found in the east as well as in the west. The largest religions of the Orient, Hinduism and Buddhism, begin their explorations with an approach to the *self* markedly different than that in the religions of the west. For Judaism, Christianity and Islam, God alone is in the beginning, and God draws all that exists out of nothingness. Beginning with the lowest of pedigrees, humanity is then summoned to the highest. Human beings are called to become selves that last into eternity with the ultimate goal of communion with God and one another. The self, philosophically speaking, has lasting metaphysical weight.

So strong is this concept of the self in the west that one of the most pervasive descriptions of the human quest at various times in Christianity, for example, has been the Beatific Vision, the seeing of God face-to-face. For this reason, Dante, when he enters into God's presence in the *Paradiso,* reports his amazement at seeing a human face in the reality of God. In Robert Bolt's *A Man for All Seasons,* when Sir Thomas More reluctantly is about to take a long-avoided oath during his trial, the force that he gives to it is that if he be not telling the truth, may he never see God in the Face.

By contrast, Hinduism and Buddhism view the human as coming forth not from nothingness, but rather from the All, from Brahman. The self as each of us now knows it is but a passing phenomenon; through the process of karma, it will dissolve as an individuality, being useful primarily as helping to determine the level of its next incarnation. At the end of the total process, the self is dissolved totally and annihilated into the All. Sometimes the self is likened in such an understanding to a drop of water that falls into the ocean. It then exists only as an infinitesimal part of the greater reality. The metaphysical weight of the individual is considerably lessened; it does not last as a self into eternity. This may in part explain the western world's intense activism since it has a metaphysical root in the formation of a lasting self.

The tendency of both Hinduism and Buddhism as they develop in history, however, is to address more attention to the significance of the self and its more immediate time-bound physical and spiritual needs. Buddhism, in fact, begins in the sixth century before the common era (B.C.E.) as something of a protest movement within its parent religion, Hinduism.

Early Hinduism had taught the sorrowful process of the wheel of successive lives (*samsara*) from which ultimate release or salvation (*moksha*) could be attained after perhaps thousands of lifetimes. Buddhism would emerge with a more practical mindset and would seek ways to introduce something of the ultimate experience of life (in Buddhism called *nirvana*) beginning in the here and now of each individual life. And while Buddhism maintained its belief in the metaphysical world view of the Hindus, it offered more immediate, even joyous, human consummation.

The Buddha (563–483), Siddhartha Gautama, was a Hindu prince and, according to legend, went forth one day from his palace and beheld Four Passing Sights (age, suffering, death and sacrifice-monkhood). Seized with a desire to know what it all meant—that is, aflame with the ultimate questions—the young Siddhartha went through a process of searching and questing remarkably like that which Kierkegaard was to describe thousands of years later. First the young prince tried out the aesthetic level, trying to intensify his pleasures. He only found that the more he clung to the physical, the less lasting happiness it could bring. He realized that it too was passing.

Next, Siddhartha tried the most extreme disciplines, moving from one excess to another. Legend reports that he fasted until his diet consisted of one grain of rice a day. This sad attempt at an "ethical" approach proved not only unsatisfying, but near disastrous.

At last, the young prince settled resolutely upon a "religious" phase. Rather than try to wrench happiness or meaning or fulfillment from either his own indulgences or disciplines, he vowed to sit beneath the bodhi tree until enlightenment came upon him. This enlightenment or *satori* came to him in the form of the Four Noble Truths:

1. Suffering pervades reality.
2. The cause of suffering is desire for the unattainable.
3. Release from suffering comes from desirelessness.
4. The only way we can approximate desirelessness is through the Eight-Fold Path of righteousness and partial or temperate renunciation.

The final goal of this whole process is that state of bliss or desirelessness, that absence of individuality alluded to previously as *Nirvana*. This Nirvana, or at least its foreshadowing, may be attained by meditation and right living on the earth.

The Buddha sought to share his peace, happiness and enlightenment with others and thus he went about preaching for over forty years, giving up much of his own calm and contentment. Thus, the great ultimate questioner was seen as living a deeply sacrificial, loving life. To that life the hundreds of millions of Buddhists are still summoned by their faith.

Even our cursory glance at Hinduism and Buddhism would indicate that the east essentially asks the same primal questions as the west; its ways of response, though, vary at times while appearing strikingly similar at others. The same can be said as we look even further to the east, to one of the religions of China. Though not as numerical in its adherents or as much a household word as Confucianism, Taoism has become an increasingly well-known and appreciated "spirituality," especially in the United States. The main document of Taoism, the *Tao Te Ching,* was either written or inspired by Lao Tzu, a Chinese thinker of the sixth century B.C.E. This *Tao Te Ching* has gone through several American editions and is one of the most popular of all Oriental books in the west today.

The Chinese religions generally provide a bridge between western and eastern sensibility. In the religions of China, for example, individual existence continues beyond death, as evidenced in the importance of ancestor worship. And yet, the intense activism of the west is not so readily found in traditional Chinese religiosity. Three themes in particular in Taoism seem to have particular relevance to western hearers or readers of the chaotic late twentieth century.

First, Taoism teaches that the *Tao* flows through all things and people, relieving them of the awful anxiety of having to define their own total significance. The obvious parallels to the "Spirit" in the west have been noted by commentators. This Tao is to be experienced not only in fullness and strength, but often in stillness and emptiness as well. Using an architectural image, the *Tao Te Ching* notes that the walls of a room actually only organize emptiness; a cup or a bowl does the same. The west often seems frantic to produce, to have people and situations always at the full, always at their peak. Taoism finds possibility and pregnancy in the seemingly dull or depressed or desolate. Let being be. Let it flow. One need not be *always* busy justifying life. If one is more patient, life will assert itself anew.

Second, the *Tao Te Ching* argues that process is more important than product in a truly human life. Tension results from the futile attempt to clutch at the product of our labors, whether they be children, works of art, projects, bank accounts or a thousand other such accomplishments. These products eventually must either take on an identity of their own, or go on without us after our death. It is not so much *what* we do as *how* we do it that counts ultimately. Thus, in a striking phrase of this small but famous text, one can work and be relaxed at the same time, for one works without the exhausting burden of utter perfection and production quotas always beckoning.

Lastly, Taoism urges flexibility in life upon its adherents. Corpses are rigid, living things supple, it insists. Unbending trees topple in high wind. Flexible, yielding ones bend and survive. One need not accept the more passive even pacifistic drift of the *Tao Te Ching* in its totality to sense the "good news" that it can provide to many a workaholic in the west.

Primitive or historical, eastern or western, the religions of the world constantly confront the ultimate realities. They seek to evoke the reality of the Holy in the lives of their faithful, through story, symbol, sacred time and space, scripture and the depth life experiences. In the process, they help their adherents to find meaning and direction. They help to provide the courage to live well and fully, while discovering something of the depths of both the human and the divine.

How Christianity in particular addresses that same task will be the question to which our consideration turns in the next part of this study.

Further Reading

Bamberger, Bernard. *The Story of Judaism* (New York: 1970).
Berger, Peter (ed.). *The Other Side of God—A Polarity in World Religions* (New York: 1981).

Eliade, Mircea. *The Sacred and the Profane* (New York: 1959).

Hamilton, Edith. *Mythology* (New York: 1969).

Hatchett, Marion. *Sanctifying Life, Time and Space: An Intro-duction to Liturgical Study* (New York: 1982).

Otto, Rudolph. *The Idea of the Holy* (New York: 1964).

Power, David (ed.). *The Times of Celebration* (New York: 1981).

Smith, Huston. *The Religions of Man* (New York: 1958).

Smith, Wilfred Cantwell. *Toward a World Theology: Faith and Comparative History of Religion* (Philadelphia: 1981).

Tyrrell, Francis. *Man: Believer and Unbeliever* (New York: 1974).

Unit Four:

The Christian Response

9

The Christ: Ultimate Questioner

"Explorations into Jesus are not only historical ex-
peditions, but the way the self asks its deepest questions."
John Shea

Christianity begins its approach to the human puzzle not in
treatises or theories, not in dogmas or even testaments.
Christianity begins to come to grips with the human mystery with
a story of one who at a given time and in a given place posed the
ultimate questions in a most acute personal way for both himself
and his hearers. And this same one—the Christ—lived out a life
that was the primal response both to what humanity is and to what
it could be.

Christianity makes a considerable claim about the figure of
Christ. That claim is both widely cosmic and intensely personal.
It is that, somehow, in the life and death, actions and attitudes of
the figure of Jesus, there is to be found the key to human meaning
and significance. And the claim is yet more: that he is the fullest
revelation of God to humanity (true God) and the fullest manifes-
tation of what humanity can be (true human).

But this being said, it should also be quickly added that main-
line Christian churches are *inclusive* in their approach to the revelation of God in Christ rather than *exclusive*. That is to say that
they maintain that God indeed can and does reveal truth in countless ways and manners and religions, but that in the figure of
Christ the revelation is fullest and normative.

Even in a so-called "secular age," the figure of Jesus is a

persistent one in literature and film and imagination. As Chicago theologian John Shea has written in *The Challenge of Jesus:*

> Jesus lived out of a transcendence which first reduces humankind to wondering silence and then to a riot of metaphors. Images explore this mystery of Jesus but in no way exhaust it. Further, Jesus-imaging is the way Western people ask the meaning of life. The many Jesuses are personal and collective searches for a cause to be committed to, a passion to be consumed by, a life that has worth and purpose. Explorations into Jesus are not only historical expeditions, but the way the self asks its deepest questions.

With the phrase "the many Jesuses," Shea has pointed to a critical problem: countless people make statements about Jesus, left and right. The Jesus of the "hot" radio preacher may appear quite different from the Jesus of a high-church sermon or of a liberationist theologian stressing Jesus' social passion. Where does one turn for what Shea calls a "controlling image" of Jesus amid all the claims and counter-claims? The main-line Christian churches (including, for example, most Baptists, Catholics, Disciples of Christ, Eastern Orthodox, Episcopalians, Lutherans, Methodists, and Presbyterians) maintain that the normative Christ is to be found in the New Testament as interpreted in the historically lived experience of the community of the Church.

If we follow this main-line approach of seeking the point of widest agreement on the Christ-question, it will be necessary to inquire what it is that constitutes this Christ as the center of meaning of living faith. For a response we will turn first to the biblical evidence, and then the report of the historical traditions of Christianity.

Scripture is always the norm for the Christian believer. But the Christian of the major traditions always reads Scripture with one eye—that is to say, one eye on the text, one on the context. God is a quite vocal God, Christianity judges—a God who speaks in word and hearts and history, in nature and relationships, even in turmoil and hardships. To limit divine revelation to only the word on a printed page—those same human words, in fact, that in our every-day experience never quite succeed in conveying a message totally—is in effect to limit God. And that limitation Christianity can never permit.

Accordingly, to ask how the figure of Christ appears in Scripture is to invite the prior question as to how the preachers and leaders and theologians and faithful people of the Christian churches approach the biblical evidence. Almost without exception, the churches agree on a modified form-critical understanding of the structuring and editing of the New Testament readings, the Gospel in particular.

In this understanding, it is known that the earliest major writings of Christianity were the epistles or letters to the churches. Once Christianity began its pincer-like spread away from Jerusalem in its first generation, it moved to the north toward Antioch and to the south toward Alexandria. The faith, largely under the leadership of the amazing Paul, spread throughout the Mediterranean Basin. It arrived first largely in coastal towns and thus began largely as an urban religion. In each town, small groups followed "the Way" (one of Christianity's earliest names). They gathered together for prayer and mutual support; they looked to such places as Jerusalem and Antioch for leadership; and they exchanged letters with other towns or churches to keep their faith alive and strong. As a result, the epistles that have survived (Romans is something of an exception) are largely topical in form, dealing with particular needs, topics and problems. The earliest epistles, such as those to the Thessalonians, come from the early 50's.

It would be a whole generation later that the first Gospels appeared. These were more systematic, comprehensive documents whose intention was to communicate the message of Christ, along with a striking portrayal of Christ as the messenger. Mark is generally regarded as the earliest of the Gospels, coming from about the year 70. Luke and Matthew come within the next decade, and John seems to be the latest, appearing near the end of the century.

There were four Gospels and not just one for a fairly simple reason. The writers had different audiences. In order to communicate the shaping and saving Word most effectively, they edited and emphasized their materials in terms of their own thematics.

Matthew, Mark and Luke are generally called the Synoptics, because they drew so readily from the same sources that their writings could be put in synopses or columns and easily compared and contrasted. John breathes a different air, as it were, taking on a more poetic style and a more Hellenistic mentality.

Matthew's audience is primarily Jewish. His genealogy traces Jesus' roots back to Abraham, father of the Jewish faith. Luke, the more universalizing writer, by contrast, traces the lineage to Adam. Matthew stresses Jesus as the new Moses, alone of all the New Testament writers reporting the flight into Egypt, paralleling the baby Moses' endangerment as a child. Matthew alone has Jesus proclaim the epochal statement of the Beatitudes from a mountain, like Moses on Sinai. Luke, almost by way of painful contrast, stresses that Jesus came into the plain to give the address.

Matthew, again the profoundly Jewish reporter, emphasizes Jesus as rabbi, as teacher. His portrayal comes closest to having Jesus in tweeds, in a professorial role. His book is set up in five major lectures delivered by Jesus, drawing together themes and remarks placed elsewhere by the other Synoptics. Each lecture or discourse (such as the Beatitude discourse in chapters 5 through 7) is preceded by a narrative section in which Jesus is active in healing, miracles, confrontations etc., often reflecting the theme of the accompanying discourse.

The Gospels reflect at times a high degree of literary construction and sophistication. In knowing the form and structure, one also comes to know more clearly the thematic and intention of the evangelist.

Accordingly, to look at chapters four and five of Matthew (as we are about to do) and investigate the temptation and Beatitude accounts, is to be fairly sure that one is approaching a pivotal section of Matthew's account. In using these sections to present a "controlling" description of Jesus, one can be fairly sure of being close to Matthew's own vision, and not merely pulling lines at random to suit one's purpose (always a dangerous procedure in any religion).

The temptation scene of Matthew (4:1–11) is particularly striking. Jesus enters the desert for a time of identity testing, "led by the Spirit." The forty days suggest the forty years of testing and formation of Moses and the Israelites after the exodus. And just as in the midst of that desert experience Moses goes up a mountain, Sinai, to strike a covenant or testament, so at the conclusion of Jesus' testing he goes up a mountain (in Matthew's account, chapter 5) to proclaim a new testament, the Beatitude discourse.

Jesus is tempted in this desert scene three times:

to turn stones into bread;

to leap from the Temple and count on a miracle for safety;

to worship Satan and all he stands for and thus to have power in the world.

Dostoevsky in his *The Brothers Karamazov* maintains that no more dramatic statement of the fundamental human life options than these three could be crafted, even if all the great thinkers of all time were brought into a room and invited to collaborate.

From an ultimate questions point of view, it might be said that Jesus is being tested on the essential meaning of life. The satan figure gives him an opportunity to fill in the blank: The basic human purpose in life is (*reply*). The tempter suggests as a first reply, *security*: the meeting of bodily needs is all that is really necessary for life. Jesus rejects this as the response, not opposing security in itself as a human need, but rejecting it as the fundamental purpose of existence.

Next the tempter suggests that *thrills,* magic, kicks, and high moments are the redeeming things about life—that one could be free of responsibilities for one's own life or that of others, and that God will somehow do it all for humanity. This, too, Jesus rejects. Not keen experience, and not the possibility of God's involvement does he turn aside, but the conviction that immediate satisfaction, selfish and irresponsible enjoyment are all that matter.

Finally, the temptation is to worship satan and all that he signifies: *meaninglessness,* pointlessness, apathy, selfishness, evil. All scruples out of the way, one might attain enormous power over all the kingdoms of the earth. And just as Jesus reverenced food, security, and joy (and made it most evident at other times) so too does he reverence power for the good. But power for its own sake, manipulative and self-serving, he casts away as an unworthy goal of human living.

In all three cases his judgment is strikingly similar. The temptations have been to short-circuit life, to keep it from being all that it can be by diminishing humanity's deepest capabilities. Jesus, the ultimate questioner of the desert, having rejected a series of false, though at times attractive, human alternatives, is now prepared to make his own first statement of life's basic drive and direction.

In the fifth chapter of Matthew, Jesus begins the first of his major lectures. In the Beatitudes discourse (Mt 5:1–12) he portrays a world turned upside down, a revolutionary perspective that has been blunted in the western world by so many years of pious listening and head-nodding in churches.

The Beatitudes announce that things are not what they seem

to be on the surface. Out front, it looks that what makes for happiness in the world is unending possession, riches, brute strength, unending jolliness, insulation from the problems of others, the venting of one's feelings whenever and wherever. Jesus' Beatitudes make it clear first of all that the fundamental human drive is rightly toward happiness. But the way to achieve true, lasting, ultimate happiness is not in a wild grab for power or money or meaning.

Blessed happiness instead has to do with having a character and identity that is not totally dependent on accumulations, that can withstand loss and testing, that is more deeply rooted in life itself. Jesus' version of happiness says that we are not what we have, or we are not just a function of what happens to us. Happiness is involved with gentleness more than with rage, with hospitality more than hostility (as Henri Nouwen phrased it), with sharing more than grasping, with concern and compassion rather than apathy and supposed self-insulation. Those who seek to build a better world—those who hunger for the right, seek justice and peace, even if they are misunderstood, opposed, crucified—these are the people most fundamentally attuned to what life should be, and what leads to genuine happiness. The discourse then continues with an array of invitatory images: to become a light in the darkness; to become the salt that seasons, preserves and stings societies. The discourse offers specifics about giving for the needs of others, about human and divine trust, and about the need for prayerfulness.

The crowds at the end of the speech, Matthew's account allows, were amazed. The teaching had made "a deep impression." And small wonder. Jesus had begun the process of showing his own approach to the fundamental human questions, and they were stunning.

The rest of Matthew's Gospel builds on this foundation, elaborating the fundamental perspective in both the words and the actions of Jesus. He not only announced, he incarnated the message, giving it the force of life and blood. And even when his basic position got him into serious trouble, he refused to back into safety and security, but paid a prophet's price. So it was that the drama at the end of Jesus's life—the suffering, the trial, the crucifixion—were consequences of the way he lived his life. The death in itself would not be remarkable without its accompanying unsurpassable affirmation of the depth of conviction with which Jesus held his primal convictions about the truer self, others, the earth and ultimately God's own being.

Throughout Matthew, the burden of teaching is often carried by the parable, a short story or little image Jesus would use to present some of the many facets of the complexity of life's fullness. There is a certain parallel in the Jewish-Christian parable to the *koan* in Zen. This latter is a short riddle or story specifically designed to shock the hearer out of the traditional way of thinking, in order to approach life from a fresh perspective. Famous and classical koans include: What is the sound of one hand clapping? What did your face look like before your mother conceived you?—madness at first to the western mind, but thresholds of awareness for the disciplined mind of the east.

The parable thrives on exaggeration. That is the very factor that makes the point. Jesus, the good teacher, the seasoned rabbi, uses so many parables that scholars call one of the five discourses in Matthew (chapter 13) the "parabolic discourse." There, through the use of parables, we find Jesus trying to describe the *kingdom,* his working symbol for the meaning and significance of human life under the trusted leadership of God.

The kingdom is dynamic; it is like the mustard seed that grows to greatness from unimpressive beginnings (13:31). The kingdom reveres the hidden greatness of the ordinary as revealed in the yeast that makes bread possible (13:33). The kingdom involves setting one's priorities straight as in the pearl in the field story (13:44). The kingdom involves insecurity and risk as in the parable of the talents (25:14).

The kingdom is presided over by a God who is like a woman who rejoices at finding a lost coin (Lk 15:8–10), or like the father in the famous story of the prodigal son who is ecstatically happy at the return of the runaway son (Lk 15:11–32), or like the shepherd who cares so much for one wayward sheep that he leaves ninety-nine others to give his intense attention to the stray (Mt 18:12–14).

These last three stories all show effectively the exaggerated dimension of the parable. To celebrate the finding of a dime—especially by a poor woman—by giving a party for the whole neighborhood is hardly sensible; nor would the shepherd's local union look kindly on his handling of the ninety-nine. And the prodigal son gets an extravagant party too, galling the other son who stayed quietly and productively at home. But the stories aren't meant to be practical; they are meant to startle. They are designed to stress just how intensely God loves and cares for each individual without exception, even to the point of the seeming passing of the bounds of good sense. That same God cares about the ninety-nine sheep and the faithful son, but the point can only be made when even the seemingly least attractive and appealing are addressed and cared for.

Scripturally, then, Jesus is the one who comes to the world so that all people may glimpse and move toward "life to the full" (Jn 10:10). He announces the famous great commandments that encapsulate so much of the Jewish and Christian traditions: the most important task we have on earth is the loving of God with all our intensities, and the second, which is on a par with the first, is the loving of others as we love ourselves (Mk 12:28–31). This passage is laden with psychological and spiritual perception. We do not love others until we effectively and properly have a sense of self-worth. Love of others—all others—is not just a matter of emotion and feeling. If loving is at its root wishing and working for the good of the other, then it is possible to love those for whom we feel no emotional attraction. And the proper love of God, self, others, the earth, are all vitally and intricately linked with one another.

Libraries of the world are filled with elaborations of the significance of Jesus. We have tried to suggest here from a rapid look at some of the biblical materials that he persists age after age in the west as the point of religious reference precisely because he is himself a fearless poser of the ultimate questions. He is himself, in fact, a question put to the Christian believer about his and her own personal approaches to life. The story of Jesus is epic; it is in some way a reflection of everyman and everywoman, since he is like us in all things, save sin (Heb 4:15).

His life, itself under threat, judgment, and condemnation, included the range of human emotions, fears and hopes. Yet he always remained united to God and to his perception of God's way and truth. In short, over the centuries, Christians have seen the story of Jesus as a life-shaping story—one in which they see something of themselves mirrored, something sparked, something hoped for.

Christian tradition preached not only the message of Jesus. It preached also Jesus as the primal messenger. The message apart from his absolutely committed life was just another collection of words. But he wedded prayer and action, ideal and compromise, trust and independence, life and death.

The two basic assertions or doctrines about Jesus in Christian tradition have been elaborated from the biblical starting point: incarnation and resurrection.

In these doctrines, as indeed in all doctrines, Christianity has tried to express through the limited medium of words, profound and timeless spiritual-human experiences—namely that, in Jesus, God enters the turmoil and excitement of the human fabric and draws it beyond itself toward the possibility of union with God's own life. This union will not diminish individuality, Christianity maintains, but ultimately enhance it. Once the individual is decidedly joined to the depth of God, that individual begins to become a self, is freed to shake off masks and false identities, and to become authentic. This is the sense of C.S. Lewis' 1956 novel *Till We Have Faces*. Throughout the novel Psyche puzzles over the silence of God and agonizes that God does not clean up the world's chaos and make truth plain. She despairs of an answer at first and suspects God—if a God there be—of cruelty. But in the end she realizes that God intends to draw the meaning of self precisely from self, a painful birth process, to guarantee that one's life with God is still truly one's own. The life task is, then, to find and develop the true face with which to meet the Face of God. Accepting the attitude and living reality of the spirit of Christ into the self, Christianity holds, allows this freedom process to flourish.

Again, a caution. The major churches of Christianity do not deny human and spiritual growth to those not consciously within the Christian family. Some may be called to fullness of awareness of Christ; others may not. But all people of the earth without exception are called to those very realities to which the Christ pointed with his life and death: freedom, holiness, hope, possibility, forgiveness, compassion, justice, the love and service of God and human-kind.

St. Athanasius (297–373) summed up the Christian statement on the incarnation in the fourth century with the succinct formula that God became human so that humanity might enter into God. St. Irenaeus (125–202) had used a now well-known phrase: "The glory of God is humanity fully alive."

God, by this Christian perception, is vitally involved in human life, even when surface appearances seem to argue against it. God is truly involved in history, but not generally in an overwhelming way: often, in fact, in ambiguity and lack of certitude—until we have faces. Thus, the universe itself is not random or faceless, and is responsive to the personal. (This is further discussed in a later chapter on prayer.) There is a *link* between God and the human—one "human enough" (true "Man") to know human brokenness and hope from within, and one "divine enough" (true God) to draw humanity from inside out from its narrowness into life to the full, into life with God. The incarnation's insistence about Jesus, then, is that he is the fullest revelation of God to the world as well as the ultimate disclosure of what humanity might be.

Vital twin to the incarnation doctrine, that God dwells among us in Jesus, true God and true human, is the teaching of the resurrection: that Jesus' life and all for which it stood continues, transferred into a new and fuller dimension of life. Furthermore, Christianity maintains that this Jesus is not alone in resurrection. He is "first born of the dead." Through his life and death, the power of resurrection is open to all people now, beginning in this life, and continuing beyond it into the fuller dimensions of life in eternity.

It was the event of the resurrection that truly began Christianity as a major religion. If it had all ended with the crucifixion, the world would have witnessed but another good life snuffed out by the forces of darkness. But the disciples of Jesus, that hard-nosed, frightened, and—it must be said—cowardly group that fled from their friend at the critical moment, experienced something so powerful together that they were willing to give up their lives rather than stop repeating the experience and its implications for the world.

That experience they felt compelled to tell, for which telling, in fact, all except John had to give their lives, was what Christianity terms the resurrection: it was an experience of their friend Jesus as living still, but in a more profound dimension of life. It was the realization that this new life was the result of—and in continuity with—the great messages he proclaimed in his life and ministry. It was also the assurance that this new life—here and hereafter—was available to all.

For Christianity, the resurrection is akin to a first promising punch against a particularly abusive enemy. It is an assault upon the empire of decay and meanness and absurdity, a kind of cosmic trump card. For this reason, Easter is Christianity's primal day, promising the persistence of life deep down, beneath seeming and semblance.

If Jesus lives still, the ancient faith of Christianity insists, then his vision of humanity is vindicated, and his perspective on God as well. The age-old questions are thus seen to meet in the Christ as at a crossroads. To say that Jesus "is Lord" is to say in part that his responses to the ultimate things make ultimate sense.

Further Reading

Adam, Karl. *The Christ of Faith* (New York: 1957).

Brown, Raymond. *Jesus: God and Man* (New York: 1957).

Hellwig, Monika. *Understanding Catholicism* (New York: 1981).

Kee, Howard Clark. *Jesus in History* (New York: 1977).

O'Grady, John F. *Models of Jesus* (Garden City, N.Y.: 1981).

Perrin, Norman, and Duling, Dennis. *The New Testament: An Introduction* (New York: 1982).

Rahner, Karl. *Foundations of Christian Faith* (New York: 1978).

Rosten, Leo (ed.). *Religions of America* (New York: 1975).

Scott, Bernard B. *Jesus, Symbol-Maker for the Kingdom* (Philadelphia: 1981).

Senior, Donald. *Jesus: A Gospel Portrait* (Cincinnati: 1975).

Shea, John. *The Challenge of Jesus* (New York: 1977).

Weaver, Mary Jo. *Introduction to Christianity* (Belmont, Cal.: 1984).

10

The Face of God

"To believe in a god means to see that the facts of
the world are not the end of the matter. To believe
in God means to see that life has a meaning."
Ludwig Wittgenstein (1889–1951)

Thus far, the investigation of the ultimate questions has led to
certain conclusions that can be painted with only the broad-
est brush. While some of these areas might still be considered con-
troversial, a significant array of literary figures, theologians,
scientists, philosophers and social scientists would have some
amount of ease with these truisms:

1. *Range of Experience.* Humanity includes within its individual
   as well as corporate scope the most extraordinary range of experiences: the ordinary, the trivial, the tragic, the terrible; the
   exciting and the exhilarating: agony and ecstasy; loneliness,
   precision, guilt, fear, peace, hope, humor; and anxiety, the terror of non-significance or non-being.
2. *Meaning Seekers.* Not content merely to observe, record, and
   predict such experiences, we are seekers of their meaning. We
   puzzle over patterns and wonder if it all—or even in part—fits
   together. We live not only on facts but on *interpretations* of
   facts, and that sets us apart on the planet earth. Our languages,
   sophisticated communications systems, diplomacies, economic structures, great works of art and pieces of literature—
   all are elaborate manifestations of the simple reality that we are
   interpreting creatures.

3. *Symbol Makers*. To know is never enough for the human restlessness. We also need to *express* what we know and what we feel. Furthermore, we need to express ourselves clearly and intensely, so that often the expression itself becomes a new and powerful experience. Thus we create symbols, languages, stories, myths, rituals—all of these pointing to mysteries, depths, and patterns within human experience that may well not be explainable by human constructs alone. That is to say, it may not be unreasonable to suspect a reality that makes the human possible, while not being limited to the human horizon. More bluntly still, the human reality may point to spirituality and divinity as part of its own ultimate explanation.

4. *Partially Free*. We discover ourselves to be creatures of limited choices, but choices nonetheless. The implications of Marx's social thought, of Freud's psychoanalysis, of Skinner's programming, would seem to be that since change is a goal, it must also be a possibility. If it is a possibility, it is also a responsibility and some modicum of choice is involved. Once we assume response-ability, we acknowledge ourselves to be moral creatures, working on principles and playing by rules not limited to physical explanations alone.

5. *Relational Beings*. We do not exist of ourselves, either physically, economically or emotionally. We are defined in some large measure by the quality of our interrelationships. We live in such a web of relationships that traditional western thought has consistently dishonored suicide as a rupturing of linkages in several lives, not as a matter of the loss of one individual alone.

This reading of the human, which is, of course, in its way, revelatory of certain perspectives, leaves vast questions unanswered. For example, can all these facts, interpretations and judgments be put together in an integrated way? It is, of course, Carl Jung's psychological perspective that human life is precisely a process of situating the self within some primal wholeness. Human lives are marked with the tasks of integration and individuation.

But Jung himself was the first to admit the complexity of the task. The human condition was well described by a line from Jim Croce's "Leroy Brown": "Leroy looked like a jigsaw puzzle with a couple of pieces gone." C.S. Lewis had a similar concept. The world would be simpler if it were either all chaos or all order, Lewis thought. But it is just ordered enough to cause us to reject utter randomness, and chaotic enough to make us bristle at simplistic accounts of ultimate order. We find ourselves back in Pascal's world: creatures in the middle, neither beasts nor angels. We are questioners who believe in the force of the question, even when we nearly despair of the answers. We live in a world that seduces us toward happiness, and then breaks our hearts. This world seems to awaken within us dreams and desires that it cannot itself satisfy. The world cannot answer its own most fundamental questions.

It is precisely at this point that Christianity begins its religious and philosophic task. Taking the life, death and resurrection of Jesus as its absolute norms, Christianity honors the world and cherishes all that is truly human within it. But taking a clue from Kierkegaard's medicinal despair, it insists that the world, real and substantial as it is, points beyond itself to something more. Once again, Martin Luther King's insight applies: we live on a colony of time but in an empire of eternity. We live profoundly in two orders, Tillich said: chronos and kairos, the timely and the timeless. Until we understand ourselves as both facts and mysteries, we fail to understand ourselves at all.

It is by entering the mystery of the Christ, Christianity consistently maintains, that we enter most fully into the mystery both of ourselves and of God. "To have seen me is to have seen the Father," Jesus boldly declares in John's Gospel (14:9). And it is within this context that we begin to examine the God of Christianity: first, an examination of the grounds for and against belief in this God; then, an examination of the attributes of the Christian God.

In July 1940, light years away from today's popular music tastes, a song arrived at the top of the charts called "Fools Rush In." Anyone approaching the subject of God's existence and attributes in a few pages must surely feel the force of that old song title. To read the survey histories of philosophy of religion, to study the arguments for and against the existence of God; to examine such major studies as Hans Küng's *Does God Exist?* (1978) or Langdon Gilkey's *Naming the Whirlwind: The Renewal of God Language* (1969), and then to attempt a summary statement—this is a foolishness indeed, even if it be a necessary one in the context here.

Although there are several reasons given for contemporary atheism, two cases are most often made against the existence of God. The first of these is the seeming absence of God from immediate experience and impact on the human situation. The second is the manifold fact of evil in the world. The first of these might be called the argument from the absence of the mystical; the second from the absence of the moral in the world. Theologians and philosophers fairly uniformly consider the moral argument against God the more powerful.

But to consider the argument from mystical absence for a moment, it reveals a situation that always has existed as a possibility within the context of faith. The great mystics and saints often reported arid times and "dark nights of the soul." But what marks off the modern condition as different is the pervasiveness of the non-experience of the presence of God in a culture that grows ever more secular, ever less attuned to religious conceptions and symbols.

After the fourth century, western culture "went Christian," so that belief was shored up by cultural support and peer acceptance. But with the Enlightenment and the drive for verification, certitude, and this-worldly experience, the situation changed starkly. But whereas some writers speak of the absence or "death" of God, other theologians report on the same experience (or lack of it) with the phrase "the eclipse of God." This concept, used effectively by Martin Buber and echoed by Gabriel Marcel, argues that humanity has blocked its access to the experience of transcendence (much as the earth blocks the sun in a lunar eclipse) by becoming depersonalized and overly technical.

To lose the preciousness of the interpersonal and the sacredness of human intimacy and relationships in a desperate effort to grow rich or successful is to blunt the best receiver we have been given to receive the signals of the divinity. This rejoinder to the argument from mystical absence would then be that God has not ceased to "broadcast," as it were; humanity has chosen to jam the communication, or has failed to listen for it altogether. This is seen as the consequence when busy-ness and franticness crowd out time for listening, reflection, and meditation.

Now to address outright the major objection to the existence of God: the evident fact of massive evil in the world. Evil is not a novelty in this century. Suffering and contradiction and the defeat of the good have been constant companions of the human experience. But the twentieth century is, after all, the century of the atomic and hydrogen bombs, of the holocaust, of two massive world wars and an unending series of smaller wars, starvations and unspeakable cruelties.

If evil is taken to be the undercutting of a person's or thing's drive to achieve its natural ends and possibilities, then it is possible to distinguish two types of evil. First is *physical* evil, the destruction of a thing's capabilities that happens without conscious intention. Thus, the damage of cancer, or a tornado, from the point of view of the sufferer, is a physical evil, harming the system, but not consciously caused by any other moral agent. Second, *moral* evil is that harm or destruction which is under the conscious control of a moral agent. Thus, presuming that the will is not negated by insanity, a conscious choice to shoot someone, or to tear down a reputation by gossip, or drink heavily and wreck a car: these are examples of moral evils—evils that need not have happened. From the point of view of the ones on whom the suffering is inflicted, the evils are perceived as physical evils as well.

The point of this distinction is to trace out the traditional philosophical and theological judgment that the "explanation" of physical evil is a more difficult case than that of moral evil. If one asks why an all-knowing, all-good and all-powerful God doesn't intervene in human events whenever one person threatens another through moral evil, the answer is somewhat straightforward: if God did not permit us to choose greater and lesser, better and worse, then God in effect would not enable us to choose at all. That is to say, the price of human freedom is the allowance of moral choice and moral evil. To deny the choice of evil is to deny freedom altogether and turn the human being into a puppet.

If this can be said to give an approach without a complete answer, it must be admitted that the case of physical evil is more complex. David Hume put the case boldly in the late eighteenth century when he suggested that a God who is all-powerful is not all-good; or if all-good, then not all powerful. If God could prevent physical evil but didn't, then the divine goodness might be questioned. And if God would stop it but cannot, then divine power is challenged.

There is a presumption in Hume's point, of course. It is that the prevention of physical evil would always be better for humanity than its allowance. Even if this be true in many cases, it cannot be said to be true in all. Some greater good might come of that which is perceived as evil. Put another way, suffering and evil are not necessarily one and the same. Suffering might lead to something greater, not only something less.

This is, in fact, the first level of response of Christianity to the problem of physical evil: suffering may bring about a greater good, and thus not ultimately be evil. An athlete knows this. So does a careful student. An athlete and, let us suppose, a language student both give up certain comforts. They sacrifice. They "suffer through" training, practice, vocabularies, grammar. They could play or loaf rather than take up the disciplines they impose upon themselves. But the discipline at last delivers: one can perform well on the playing field or in fluently speaking or reading an entirely new language. Discipline and suffering, often perceived as evils, can, in fact, be hidden opportunities for good.

At a second level of response, the western religions suggest that life itself can be compared to a birth process. It is often full of pain and insecurity and even trauma. But the result is the coming into being of a full, chosen, conscious life. Another example might be the attaining of a college degree. If one could purchase a diploma in the college business office, but without all the attendant study, struggle, grades, socializing, fun and perplexities of college years and experience, that diploma would be utterly phony. Such a diploma would not rightly be one's own; it wouldn't have the smudge and smell and mark of the self upon it. And so, the argument goes, with life. It must truly be made one's own as one comes to birth in maturity; that means risk, mistakes, growth, diminishment, achievement and change.

But there are times and situations that eventually seem to touch every life in one way or another—times when these answers don't completely satisfy, times when comforters can't do much comforting. A child is dying of leukemia. An adolescent life is crushed out in a freak traffic accident. The innocent suffer in war. Does Christianity lose its voice when it hits such bottom lines?

This third level of response to the problem of physical evil reveals the way the Christian concept of God is colored by its presentation through the figure of Jesus. Christianity's primal sign is that of the cross, of an innocent who suffered. Many of the other great world spiritualities, Hinduism and Buddhism in particular, center around the problem of evil and symbolize themselves accordingly (the wheel of suffering and samsara in the east).

Jesus faced the problem of intractable suffering, both moral and physical, head-on. His very last words from his cross of execution were of a well-known Jewish psalm, showing once again the profound Judaism of Jesus. "My God, my God, why have you abandoned me?" begins the twenty-second psalm; but the psalm ends with a thumping assertion of trust in God despite all present appearances. And so Christianity responds to intractable evil by pointing to the resurrection, the undoing of evil from inside out.

Without facile dismissal of the frightful realities of pain and depression and oppression, Christianity argues that each individual was made ultimately for happiness. That process is open to all, if not in the obviousness of the here and now, then beyond even death itself. For resurrection, as discussed in the last chapter, argues that death is a process, not a finality.

"For your faithful people," the Roman funeral liturgy reads, "life is changed, not taken away." Death itself is regarded as a kind of birth process into a fuller, continuous dimension of existence. Jesus Christ, the "first born of the dead," is seen as the model marcher on that dark passage. And far from making all of this an invitation to passivity or withdrawal from life and struggle, Christianity uses it to invite humanity to the struggle that alone gives beatitude and peace: the struggle for integrity, justice, peace, endurance and preciousness of life.

There are even those who argue within Christianity that in some sense the resurrection is an answer to all prayer (this subject of prayer will be taken up in a later chapter). If, in fact, all the needs that we pour out in petitionary prayer are the present manifestations of the wider drives that we possess for a removal of frustration and limitations, then the only ultimate answer to such requests is an undergirding power that opens each to life freely and absolutely. To that power, Christianity gives the name resurrection.

In summary, Christianity argues about physical evil that, as central as our physical environment and well-being may be to each and all of us, we are ultimately more than the physical. The physical is subsumed in each of us, taken into something more fundamental still, an identity, a dimension, a reality not limited to the physical. In this inner core, at the center of choice and intimate identity—the core which we only gradually and carefully reveal to special friends and lovers throughout our lives, because it is our most vulnerable self—*there* is the non-physical principle that makes all our physicality have significance. There, too, Christianity will argue, God is present, heart to heart, beneath all seemings and surface appearances.

Having looked at two major arguments against the existence of God, we turn now to a consideration of the other side of the case. Traditionally in western philosophy, four types of argument have surfaced in support of the existence of God. The God thus supposed to be proved is not necessarily co-extensive with the developed conceptualization of the personal God of Judaism, Christianity or Islam, but the Primal Cause and Intelligence of the universe. The four types of argumentation have been:

1. *Cosmological.* Beginning with the evident facts of motion and change, one argues that—disallowing an infinite series of physical things ad infinitum—there must be a first cause, unmoved mover, or first necessity in a world of contingency. Cosmos prevails over chaos. There is a source of this cosmos: thus it is called the "cosmological" argument.

   Possible Objection: The proof is based on a presumption of what Küng calls a fundamental trust in reality in the first place. Can it really be proved that an infinite regress is impossible?

2. *Teleological.* Telos is a Greek word meaning end or purpose. The teleological argument takes note of the many evidences of order in the world, especially in the realms of biology, chemistry, and astronomy, and argues that such order could not be

accidental. There must have been a primary orderer or giver or end or purpose to such things. Like the cosmological argument, this one is heavily based on the thought of Aristotle and amplified by Thomas Aquinas.

Possible Objection: Even leaving aside the painful amount of disorder to be found in the world (as examined in the section on evil), the theories of evolution coming from the nineteenth century provide at least an alternate explanation for order rather than disorder, in some sense—namely, that which is more "ordered" or complex merely survived; it wasn't planned.

3. *Ontological.* Probably the most difficult of the arguments, it is usually associated with the figure of Anselm (1033–1109). Working from the *idea* of God as the most perfect and necessary being, one might argue that since the idea is itself a reality, and since perfection is part of the idea, and since existence in fact is greater than existence in mere idea, then there in fact exists a perfect being reflective of our innate idea of one.

Possible Objection: Besides the subtlety of the case, the main problem has been the making of the leap from an idea of a God to a fact of one.

4. *Moral.* Especially significant for such diverse thinkers as Kant and Newman, the moral argument builds on the evident fact of our inner awareness of the "world of the ought," non-physical, but profoundly real. What is the source of such a reality, if not the creation of God?

Possible Objection: The moral argument is a forceful one, but has been challenged by both analytic philosophers and some social scientists on the grounds that moral imperatives are really only disguised social pressures.

There are other arguments, of course, though they are not usually presented with the same philosophic rigor as the classical four. These, not necessarily the less significant, are more existential in their scope. One such argumentation is *the mystical,* from the profound inner experience of the individual. This was of special interest to a William James, for example, or a Carl Jung. There is also the phenomenon of the persistence of religious experience and thought in all times and cultures that would seem to argue either for some validity of the experience of God or else a massive human delusion as an alternative. This might be called the *cultural* argument.

American sociologist Peter Berger in an intriguing short study titled *A Rumor of Angels* (1969) suggests that even in our secular age we have what he calls "signals of transcendence." These are everyday experiences that point, presumably, to some order or coherence in the structure of the universe itself. If coherence is established, then a conception of God is much more plausible than not, Berger judges. The five signals are the human propensities for order, play, hope, righteous anger and humor.

Even if the word "chaotic" might best describe the room we call most specially our own, practically everyone has some minimal sense of order: of occasionally setting a chair right side up, of balancing a checkbook, of doing dishes before the Board of Health arrives. Most people have at least some vestige of a sense of humor and play that enables them to stand outside themselves a bit—to transcend, that is, go beyond the obvious and the ordinary. Similarly, when we get angry over a slight or an injustice, we point, however modestly, to some structure of meaning in reality. If everything was random, chaotic, utterly devoid of purpose other than that we inflict upon it, would hope and human resiliency in spite of all obstacles (even and especially in concentration camps) make any sense at all? And yet our surest psychological instincts tell us that these very experiences are fundamental to psychological health. They cannot be lightly dismissed. Berger doesn't overrun his argument; his "signals" are pointers, not proofs. But they point beyond business as usual and beyond the physical and the obvious as the horizon of our beings.

The Christian churches generally lean on a philosophic background to situate their message. Some traditions (such as the Roman Catholic and Episcopal) are historically close to natural law and philosophic underpinnings. Others, such as the Neo-Orthodox or Evangelical, are more uneasy with the input of the reasoning function into the life of faith. Reason and experience can take us part of the way at least, most traditions would allow in some sense, but not the full way into the most critical insights about self, life, and God. In the greatest of medieval poems, Dante's *Divine Comedy*, Virgil, the symbol of reason, leads Dante through the other world only to a certain level. Above that, Beatrice and Bernard, symbols of saintliness, take over.

In the fullest sense, God cannot be known by the reason alone. The reasoning faculty may point the human toward coherence, order, creation or higher intelligence. It may show, as St. Thomas Aquinas (1224–1274) said, *that* God is, but not *what* or *who* God is. Partly that is because of the immensity of God, but also it is because our reasoning faculty is only one of several ways of human knowing. To know only through reason is not to know in the most penetratingly existential human way. The most complete way of knowledge is not just mental connection, Christianity says; it is interconnection, intercommunion. In a word, the ancient faith maintains, the fullest knowing is in loving. And God *is* love.

And so Christianity came to describe the attributes of God as Jesus understood and revealed them: a God who is both Alpha and Omega for humanity, the beginning and the end, the One who first calls into being, and who then calls each individual further into self-being—into a faced, personal, unique existence in communion with others and with God.

The God of Christianity is perceived as not just *a* limited person, but hyper-personal, calling into being the mystery of the human. This same God comforts, quickens (to use the old Episcopal term), but also challenges the individual to break out of narrowness, isolation, and sin.

This God who is the Ground of mercy, knowledge, justice, and compassion may well be often a hidden God, lying in wait in Emily Dickinson's "fond ambush." This God, with aspects of Father and Mother, can draw possibility and hope out of despair and seeming desolation.

As opposed to Marx's oppressive god, the God of Christianity is perceived as liberating societies and selves. And over against Freud's projection god, the God of this historic faith is a God of surprises, often a Lord of insecurities that invite new self-discoveries. This God can be said to be present to the core-identity of each person constantly, uniquely and intimately.

Christianity refers to this God as Trinity: Father, Son and Holy Spirit. Thereby, Christianity suggests, among other things, at the heart of God is dynamism, interpersonal relationship and intense energy. God is at once so immense, so vast, yet so simple, that the divinity is not exhausted in isolated personhood but subsists in a community of persons.

Since the beginnings of the nineteenth century, the conception of God has not only been challenged outside Christianity and the other western faiths. It has been reformulated within Christianity as well. Thus, Kant deemphasized what we can know of God, stressing the moral route as the only sure one with reference to the deity. Hegel stressed God as immanent and dynamic rather than changeless, and helped set a theme that would be elaborated in the twentieth century.

Friedrich Schleiermacher (1768–1834) portrayed a God who

was the Whence of human feeling and ultimate dependence. This God intervenes little in the human and is less seen as challenge than as a kind of cosmic support. In some ways influenced by the German Protestant Schleiermacher, "the father of modern theology," were process thinkers who saw God as an immanent, limited force for development. Included in this line of thinkers would be William James (1842–1910), John Stuart Mill (1803–1876) and in this century Alfred Whitehead (1861–1947).

Paul Tillich (1886–1965), a Lutheran theologian, in some ways wedded the thought of many of the thinkers previously mentioned and named God as "Ultimate Concern" or "Ground of Being," fearing that the very word "God" may be confusing in the modern world. Catholic theologian Karl Rahner (1904–1984) pictures a God who is first known through the existential drive of human nature to transcend itself. Jesus, Rahner says at one point, was the one who was able to say "Father to incomprehensibility."

Protestant theologians in the twentieth century have ranged from Karl Barth, who emphasized God as revealed in Christ alone, to Dietrich Bonhoeffer (1906–1945), who spoke of the falseness of a God pushed to the fringes of life, a "stopgap" God simply used to explain our unknowns. Bonhoeffer spoke of "religionless Christianity" and helped to spark the "Death of God" school of theology quite prominent in the middle and late 1960's, but little in evidence thereafter.

The purpose of this "hit and run" raid on the God image in several major modern theologians is to suggest how wide-ranging the question of God is even (and especially) within the Christian churches today.

Divisions fall not so much along denominational as along theological lines. And still, even granted the differences among many sincere thinkers trying to be "honest to God" in an age of confusion, rapid change, and at times desperation, there is still something recognizable about the earlier portrayal of God given above to most of the Christian churches today.

God perceived as creative source, comfort, challenge, judge, lover, parent, hope, and destiny—these are among the fundamental things that apply in Christianity, in and out of theological season.

Further Reading

Adler, Mortimer. *How To Think about God: A Guide for the 20th Century Pagan* (New York: 1980).

Chapman, Colin. *The Case for Christianity* (Grand Rapids: 1981).

Gilkey, Langdon. *Naming the Whirlwind: The Renewal of God Language* (Indianapolis: 1969).

Gilkey, Langdon. "The Idea of God Since 1800," in *Dictionary of the History of Ideas* (New York: 1973), Vol. II. pp. 354–66.

Hick, John. *Evil and the God of Love* (San Francisco: 1978).

Küng, Hans. *Does God Exist?* (New York: 1978).

Murray, John C. *The Problem of God* (New Haven: 1964).

Rahner, Karl. *Do You Believe in God?* (New York: 1969).

Schilling, Paul. *God and Human Anguish* (Nashville: 1977).

Tillich, Paul. *The Shaking of the Foundations* (New York: 1948).

11

Transformations:
The Consequences of Belief

"Brooding on God, I may become a man."
Theodore Roethke (1908–1963)

Earlier, in describing the four essential components of all religion, we commented on creed, code, ceremony and community. In this unit of consideration of Christianity's response to ultimate questions, we have centered attention so far on basic creedal positions—on overall approaches to the nature of self, humanity and God. It is time now, in a shorter compass, to examine the other components of the Christian religion, and to check their bearing on the ultimate things.

Immediately upon the dramatic events at the end of Jesus' life—the trial, execution and resurrection—a community of faith formed to draw strength from all that Jesus had been, had stood for, and had now become. They wished not only to let the Spirit nurture them in this faith; they sought also to share this saving, shaping, healing message with others.

We have already noted that the original starting point of this community, this *ecclesia* (Greek signifying a group called forth with a purpose), this Church, was an intense experience of the resurrection. In order to share the mystery and force of that resurrection, the message of ultimate deliverance from sin, limitation, meaninglessness and death itself, the disciples were willing to offer up their own lives.

Most of the early Christians, at least in the first generation of faith, were people who went their quiet way, still considering themselves part of Judaism, worshiping in the temple or synagogue and then going to a private home to celebrate the Eucharistic meal of Jesus. (It was not until the fourth century when Christianity ceased being a hunted and persecuted religion and became the state religion of the empire that church buildings began to appear.) There emerged a small group of leaders in the early Church, especially in Jerusalem and Antioch. The apostles Peter and James were looked to for special leadership. Roman Catholicism in particular has always looked to the succession of Peter at Rome as a special symbolization of the authority of the Church.

A very small number of the followers of "the Way" were missionaries to the far-flung empire, foremost among them, of course, the dynamic Paul of Tarsus. He had originally been most likely a Pharisee and a persecutor of the early Church. In an exceedingly dramatic moment of revelation and insight, he was converted to the faith, and Christianity was never again the same. A new energy began to pervade the small and scattered communities as Paul preached throughout the Mediterranean basin, universalizing the appeal of the Gospel message. In Paul, most decisively, Christianity saw itself as a universal religion for Jew and Gentile, slave and free, male and female.

These Christian communities grew, fending off persecution without and heresies within. Among these latter was Gnosticism which argued for private revelations and spiritual elitism to the exclusion of Scripture, tradition, community and respect for the physical. Another early heresy was Arianism that looked upon Jesus as the highest of creatures, but not truly as being of the substance of God. Against the heresies, the early Church reacted with the elaboration of creeds, the settlement on the accepted books of the New Testament, and an emphasizing of the heritage of bishops as witness of the apostolic tradition.

Throughout all of these tumultuous times, the early Church struggled to keep alive a coherent view of life's purpose and energies. The Church in fact could be described as that movement of people in history who found in the Christ the centerpoint of their own and the world's significance. They believed in the potential goodness of all people, but they also held that by entering into the life, perspective and power of the still-living, risen Christ, the individual could become part of God's own life.

C.S. Lewis once used this analogy to explain the Christian concept of the believer becoming a child of God: A person might produce a work of art and it would reflect the personality of the artist in a wonderful way. But when a couple produce a child, even more wonderfully does reality reflect the personalities and identities of the child's "creators." All people by nature are the work of God, as the art to the artisan. Those who become children of the Father by making Jesus their brother are the work of God in a more special way, as sharing his own special familial life.

This Church, proclaiming the highest of human destinies, went its way in history, becoming more dominant as the structures of the Roman Empire crumbled. Christianity served as a rallying point for what little culture and science remained in the early Middle Ages; and in the high Middle Ages it helped to produce the great universities and cathedrals, besides offering its timeless message of grace, service, prayer and virtue. In these years also, the Church became victimized by its own newfound power and success, and often seemed to be like a messenger which had forgotten its fundamental message. Partly for this reason, the western Church (centering on Rome rather than on the patriarchates of Jerusalem, Alexandria and Antioch), already divided off from the eastern Church in the eleventh century, underwent the further internal division into Protestant and Catholic groupings from the sixteenth century on.

At the end of the eighteenth century, the Church entered yet another epoch as the intimate linkage of Church and state begun under Constantine and Theodosius in the fourth century was severed in the light of the American and French revolutions. The process that is now known as secularization had begun, with vast consequences for education, politics and behavior. One somewhat unexpected consequence of secularization is that once the churches were separated from establishment with the state, they could act more as free moral agents in criticizing the economic, political and social structures of society in the light of the Gospel vision of human dignity and destiny.

The Church, in the wide sense of the term as we have been using it here, must be said to have many components. All too many people still continue to think of Church only as a building or as institutional structures. Ideally, the Church can be described as serving however imperfectly each of the following functions; with each function we will list also one of the original ultimate questions posed in chapter one as evidences of the linkage of the Church and the ultimate human concerns:

1. *Shaping Function.* In a world where clarity is at a discount, and in which there are countless ways for us to waste our human energies and potentials, religious faith offers focus, a protection against formlessness and insignificance. The Word preached by Christianity represents a steady summons to human responsibility and dignity.
   ### *Ultimate Question One: Purpose*

2. *Significance Function.* The Church is the place where the Christ is proclaimed as the centerpiece of human meaning. In his attitudes and approaches to life, self, others, earth and God are to be found a keystone of human interpretation.
   ### *Ultimate Question Two: Meaning*

3. *Preaching Function.* In season and out, the Church proclaims the Word as recorded in Scripture and as mediated through deep and diverse human experience. In pulpit, counseling, and in the example of saintly personalities, Christianity seeks to

communicate the persistence of the saving, loving reality of God let loose in the world.

Ultimate Question Three: Divinity

4. *Community Function.* The Church has a "vertical" dimension, linking the individual to God in grace at the Lord's call, and a "horizontal" dimension, as well. In this latter, the individual is joined to a community of people who share together the depth experiences of their lives in a context of Gospel faith and meaning. It is a place for the sharing of pain, diminishment, and sorrow as well as of hopes and possibilities. Always, faith points to the stance of Jesus in both suffering and triumph.

Ultimate Question Four: Pain

5. *Worship Function.* Christianity performs one of its most critical tasks when it leads its adherents to consistent prayerfulness, taking the time to situate their lives in the wider context of the reality of God. Worship draws the individual forth from selfishness, and into the power of being. Thus, worship provides an inexhaustible ground of hope in the midst of many reasons to give in to depression and despair.

Ultimate Question Five: Hope

6. *Identity Function.* The Church calls to individuals to seek out their own uniqueness, their talents, and at the same time their tasks in the wider world. It summons people away from selfishness and vice toward growth, development and virtue. Again, its call takes the form of words and sacraments, as well as living examples. Church also links the self to a network of personalities much vaster than the self: those before us in history who have shared our human drives and Christian perceptions, and those who will come after us as well.

Ultimate Question Six: Character

7. *Sacramental Function.* Most of the major Christian churches employ sacraments as part of their worship and ritual. These sacraments are manifestations of the presence of God through physical, tangible, human realities. Accordingly, Christianity must show forth the realities it refers to in flesh and blood; it must "make love visible." It must be a visibility point for the world of those hidden realities that are now seen, as Paul said, "through a glass darkly." If the world is to be more just, more sharing, more care-ful of its resources, then Christian people and institutions should provide leadership.

Ultimate Question Seven: Resources

8. *Ethical/Prophetic Function.* The Gospel not only comforts; it also unsettles. It can invite tenderness, but it also at times demands toughness. It accepts the hard reality of sin, of falling far from the ideal, or turning from the light and seeking out meanness and darkness. It calls individuals and societies to judgment unrelentingly. And if it is functioning truly as Church, it allows itself too to be subjected to criticism and judgment of its diligence, methods, leadership. As a gathering of sinners, seeded with the possibility of saintliness, the Church needs criticizing; but as carrying the Word of God, as Hans Küng points out, it is supremely worth criticizing.

Ultimate Question Eight: Morality

The Church, then, often in its stumbling way, invites people to love, to serve, to worship and ultimately to know true happiness. And if the institutional body does not communicate its message at all times effectively, it might be like the awkward parent who in faltering ways tries to impress upon an uncomprehending child quite valid insights and values. Only later, perhaps, with the lapse of time, experience and the coming of maturity, will an appreciation of at least some of the parent's message settle in. Leonard Cohan's *Suzanne* "shows you where to look among the garbage and the flowers.'' Christianity, carrying its treasures at times in the most earthen of vessels, often does precisely the same.

Paradoxically enough, one of the most important things Christianity does for its adherents is to make them conscious of sin. Students who have grasped the essential meaning of Kierkegaard and his judgment that we cannot begin to get better until we realize the extent of our sickness will not be surprised that Christianity sets such a task for itself. Ever respecting the self and the world as grounded in goodness, Christianity knows that they can go far afield from what they ought to be.

People sin. They do not just fail to develop or suffer from bad social structures. They choose lesser things when greater things are possible. They deny and undercut their own potentialities and those of others. They give in to selfishness, narrowness, meanness, and at times to brutality and cruelty. The Greek word for sin is striking: *hamartia,* an archery reference; it means ''missing the mark.'' Those who sin miss the point of what they are and what they are meant to be. Sinners misplace their loves, their values and their intensities. In its opposition to sin, then, Christianity is not repressive; it seeks to foster and unleash the best of the human powers.

T.S. Eliot (1888–1965) grasped quite well the ambiguity of the human situation and its struggle to be virtuous even as sin makes its alluring call. Sin, he knew, isn't sin just because it might be appealing or fun. God doesn't set moral obstacle courses. Sin is sin because it is a deliberate unraveling or tearing to shreds the fabric of the human and its grounding in the divine. Later we shall examine the seven ''deadly sins'' in some detail. But for now, we note Eliot's reminder in *Choruses from the Rock* (1934) that we never stand far from the moral brink:

Do you need to be told that whatever has been, can be still?
Do you need to be told that even such modest attainments

As you can boast in the way of polite society
Will hardly survive the Faith to which they owe their
significance?
Men! Polish your teeth on rising and retiring;
Women! Polish your fingernails:
You polish the tooth of the dog and the talon of the cat.
Why should men love the Church? Why should they love her
laws?
She tells them of Life and Death, and of all that they would
forget.
She is tender where they would be hard, and hard where they
would like to be soft.
She tells them of Evil and Sin and other unpleasant facts
They constantly try to escape from the darkness outside and
within
By dreaming of systems so perfect that no one will need to be
good.
But the man that is will shadow
The man that pretends to be.

The even more fundamental drive of Christian faith than
awareness of sin is the task of heightening awareness of virtue.
Sin may well be evidenced by certain actions or failures to act (as
recorded in the classical Ten Commandments), but sin is even
more: it is an orientation or fundamental stance toward self, life,
others and God.

Sin is more often a complex of attitudes and orientations than
isolated acts. Correspondingly, virtue is not a single act either.
Virtue is a habit of doing good, so that the good chosen becomes
habitual, almost "second nature."

The fundamental principle of Christian morality is deceptively simple: do good and avoid evil. And how determine good
from evil? Again, an answer that startles by its simplicity: attend
to the Gospels read in the context of wide Christian experience,
and to right reason.

Christianity speaks of original sin and suggests thereby in part that we are all born into a situation in life already corroded by sinful and selfish choices; we soon add our own strands to the net of false choices stretched under the human condition. Many Christian moral theologians speak also of mortal, serious, or venial sins as categories of severity, levels of shutting oneself off from the redemptive love of God, from the community, and from one's better self.

What's more, the Christian faith, especially in the new political situation of the last two centuries, has been especially keen on causing the faithful to recognize that there they may well be implicated in social as well as individual sin. Thus, such questions—none of them simple in themselves—as nuclear weapons, war and peace, civil and human rights, the care of the unborn, the elderly, the environment, appear on the thoughtful citizen's moral agenda.

The study of ethics in general and Christian morality in particular is a vast one. We will conclude the discussion of this chapter with a fairly simple listing, first of the traditional "seven deadly sins" and then of the seven traditional virtues. In each case, a small explanation will accompany the listing. This is intended as a portrayal of one aspect at least of the vice or virtue. In no case is it meant as an exhaustive explanation.

The Seven Capital or Deadly Sins

These seven, which were listed by writers even in the early medieval period, are sometimes called the "capital" sins because they are the "caput" (Latin: head) from which all other evils flow. One would look in vain, then, even for such enormities as murder or major theft on such a list. Rather these capital sins are the fundamental attitudes and approaches toward life from which the specific evils flow. These habits of life create an environment in which particular sins find it easy to thrive.

1. Pride

In Dante's amazing *Purgatorio,* the proud are portrayed as bearing on their backs heavy weights; they are bowed down, their vision reduced to the ground beneath them. In life they saw only themselves, and that in a false way. Now they must become humble by facing the *humus,* the earth, before they are able to experience a proper vision of reality.

Pride, then, in Christian understanding, is *not* the same as a proper sense of self-worth. Rather, it is the primal refusal to see oneself properly in the total scheme of things. Classically, pride means setting one's self up as the only being of final importance in the world. It means that the self tries to force reality into becoming the self's own reading of it. The proud love the proper thing—but in an improper way.

2. Envy

As Americans we tend to be loose in our usage of language. We might say that we wish we had a car or a suit or a sound system like someone else's, and then conclude that we are envious or jealous. Actually, the element that turns such desiring into envy is the wishing that we had such a desirable commodity and the other person did not. In other words, envy builds up one's own good or reputation at the expense of another's. The only way envious persons see that they might become large is by causing others to seem small. In a way analogous to the proud, the envious desire the proper things, perhaps, but in improper ways.

3. Anger

We live in an Age of Wrath. So writes Henry Fairlie in *The Seven Deadly Sins Today.* An incredible amount of time and energy and often violence is spent in anger in this tortured century. Individuals may be angry with other individuals, with political or ethnic groups, with social systems or governments. They may also be angry with religion, tradition, their parents, with God and ultimately even with themselves.

When Christianity speaks of anger, it does not mean merely the emotion of "getting mad," a feeling that may at times be inevitable anyway. Instead, the question that Christianity poses is the way in which such anger is directed. Is it about something worth getting angry about and worth seeking reconciliation or change? Is such anger properly channeled, or does it spew forth scatter-shot? Often, the religions remind us, we burn over something of petty personal consequence (for example, if someone makes a wisecrack about our hair or clothes) while we turn our attention steadily away from those issues in self and society worth taking on for the bettering.

4. Sloth

Remarkably it is often necessary to begin these explanations by specifying what the various sins are *not*. Sloth or laziness has nothing to do with some late morning sleep-ins or perhaps even with a "laid-back approach" to life. Sloth means something much more profoundly disturbing. It is this: the individual gives up on life, on responsibility, on personal development. Such a person opts not for direction, but for drifting as a way to live a life. Christianity argues that without some level of primary motivation, life will not just fail to reach for a pattern; it will unravel.

5. Avarice or Greed

Those who fall victim to greed, if they consider themselves Christians, may eventually have to confront Jesus' first beatitude as we examined it in Matthew's Gospel: Blessed are the poor in spirit, those who do not need to clutch at possessions or status or finances or degrees to define who they are.

Greed does not mean wanting some of the good things of the

earth and the society; it is not opposed to levels of security. But greed does mean that one is owned and defined by possessions rather than owning them. The avaricious turn away from a sharing of the goods of the earth and the fruits of production in order to clutch and accumulate such things. Thus, the ancient faith argues, they often try to avoid coming to grips with the deeper realities that could go toward constituting who they are.

6. Gluttony

Gluttony, like lust which follows in this listing, is a particular type of greed. Gluttony presents the familiar situation in which an individual places his or her most important appreciation of life in food and drink alone. People seriously caught up in gluttony, as in lust, are at the same time trapped in Kierkegaard's aesthetic level of life in which they try to force the physical to be their all-sufficiency. As many commentators have pointed out (Fairlie among them), gluttony suggests an overbearing concern with the body, a desperate attempt to make of it alone all that we can ever expect to be. Gluttony also bears a special insensitivity in a world of limited and badly distributed food and energy resources.

7. Lust

The placing of *all* one's happiness in sexual satisfaction, especially when it is promiscuous and lacking in personal and lasting commitment—that is the basic meaning of Christianity's portrayal of lust. The most damaging thing about lust (as suggested by Rollo May in an earlier chapter) is that it robs sexuality of its own most intimate and humane powers. Precisely because sexuality is so powerful a force for the good, it can be badly used, abused, manipulated. It can most readily become a fertile ground for self-deception.

Some of the early Church writers added an eighth deadly sin which did not make the final listing of the Capital Seven. This first runner-up of the deadly sins they called *tristitia* or glumness. Its opposite is *laetitia,* a happiness that supports and encourages the good, the kindly, the significant. Laetitia builds up. Tristitia tears down—not by a devastating assault, but by a slow draining of the zest for living and action.

Inside Christian moral theology today there are some who would maintain that one of our worst modern evils is the failure to nurture the strengths in individuals and societies. Seen from this angle of vision, such failure to encourage ends by failing to allow the flow of additional good into the world.

The Seven Traditional Virtues

Our English word *virtue,* sexist though it may be, comes from the Latin *vir,* gender man or masculine man. The word *virile,* of course, comes from this same root. For the classical world, then, the virtues were those habits or qualities of life that made one "manly." Not surprisingly, the stress in the Latin period was on the virtues particularly appropriate to a military environment.

In today's more sensitized understanding, the virtues are those very qualities that amplify, widen or deepen our humanity. As Christianity takes these virtues over into its own understanding, it finds a love and passion for the good at the root of each, just as each vice has manifested a love either perverse or misdirected.

1. Faith

As we saw in considering such figures as Kierkegaard and Newman, faith for Christianity involves more than a mere intellectual acceptance of credal statements. The cognitive aspect, of course, is involved in the definition of faith. Faith means a fundamental way of perceiving reality that involves the total or comprehensive self: mind, heart and will. It implies both security as well as risk, gift as well as task.

Faith involves a personal trust in the coherence of reality as a starting point. It posits the possibility of ultimate human wholeness and a final union with a God who is the Ground of all hope. Faith links together a chain of confidence that calls for a level of trust in self, others and the divine.

2. Hope

In Greek mythology, when Pandora opens the box from which all human evils are said to spring, only one good thing is said to be left to the human: hope. The virtue of hope implies a stance toward life that seeks and makes available new possibilities, even (and especially) in the midst of turmoil, frustration or disintegration. Hope represents a sustaining drive that keeps the self and others going in good times and in bad.

Especially in the midst of the depressions of the twentieth century, with its wars, holocausts, nuclear threats and depersonalizations, Christian hope reminds believers that the fundamental ground of hoping is not in the human enterprise alone. Rather, God, in the resurrection of the Christ, has tendered a promise to humanity that transcends all the evil humanity might manage to fling in its path.

3. Love

The average American is said to use the word "love" thirteen times a day—everything from "I just love bourbon candy" to "I will love you always." Love is perhaps our most difficult word to define. It ranks among such other mystery words as "why," "ought," or "promise." That hasn't kept people from trying: everyone from song lyricists to greeting card writers to St. Paul's famous definition in 1 Corinthians 13.

Love signifies our fundamental dynamism to break out of our isolation and narrowness and be joined to others. In this, love clearly is parallel to religion's task of bridging the self to the primal. As reported out by such an insightful philosopher and observer of things human as St. Thomas Aquinas, love involves willing and working for the good of another. It means, at its highest level, joy in the existence of another, not just for what the other can bring to me, but in sheer delight of the other.

Love, as suggested by such twentieth century Christians as Dorothy Day and Martin Luther King, may need to be tough at times as well as tender. Love can make demands because it seeks excellence rather than mediocrity. To love, for Christianity, is to enter into the central dynamic of God's own life; truly to love another is to wish to join him or her in the searching scrutiny, the intensity and the fullness that is the very life of God.

4. Prudence

The first three virtues just studied have traditionally been called the "theological virtues," because they invite the human into the graced world of *theos*, of God. The four now under consideration have been called the cardinal ("hinge") virtues on which other life stances turn. These were well known to the Greeks and Romans and have, in some sort, been "baptized" by the Christians. We look at them briefly here.

Prudence involves having a sense of the sensitivities both of self and others. Timing is as important in life as it is in music or athletics, and prudence turns the attention to proper timing in our human relationships. A prudent parent or friend knows just when to encourage, when to correct or suggest change.

Also, prudence is concerned with the human need to establish goals and priorities, so that direction may outrun drift in our lives. But it also signifies having the flexibility to adjust planning to realities.

5. *Justice*

This is another basic term in any personal, philosophic or civic vocabulary. It is notoriously hard to pin down, but has traditionally been described as giving to each his or her own due. For the Christian faith it carries with it the connotation of a proper sharing and shepherding of the resources that God has bestowed upon the earth. It is seen as a virtue that concerns itself with everything from civil, racial, ethnic, human, animal and environmental rights on a community or international level. But it also encompasses one's personal dealings and the way in which they respect the dignity and property of the immediate others in our lives.

6. *Temperance*

This virtue argues for the famous Aristotelian mean: moderation in all things. Virtue for Aristotle was always a middle between two extreme paths in life. Thus, courage was a middle way between rashness on one side and cowardice on the other. The temperate person seeks balance, even while feeling the pull of both sides of a tension.

Several commentators of late have suggested that one of the greatest needs for temperance in this culture and this century could well be getting Americans to turn aside from some of their desperate drivenness or workaholism. Temperance, which in an earlier age was primarily associated with turning from alcohol, could (without losing a concern for alcoholic abuse) thus be seen as a care for a balanced life-style blending work and relaxation creatively.

7. *Courage*

Ernest Hemingway called courage "grace under pressure." The word comes from a root word *cor* meaning heart. To help another person to find courage is to help in a discovery of heartiness—the quest of the Lion in *The Wizard of Oz*.

Courage means having something to stand for, and then standing for it. Additionally, courage means a basic orientation of strength or character to meet whatever comes into a life with calmness, resolve and dignity. To have courage in a religious sense implies that we are more than just the accumulation of those things that happen to us. We are in part defined by our response to such realities, and the God of mystery stands present to our own personal mystery as we face the complexity and allure of life.

Just after the Second World War, a University of Chicago professor, Richard Weaver, wrote an intriguing little book titled *Ideas Have Consequences*. It was his way of showing that the world had not outgrown the need for philosophy. Rather, he thought, unexamined and uncriticized ideas are often more dangerous than the ones we think we know.

This chapter has been an attempt to show that as far as Christianity is concerned, belief has consequences too—perhaps radical consequences. (For those few who might need reminding, radical comes from Latin *radix* for root.) After this "hit and run" raid on some of the moral consequences of Christian faith for individuals and societies, we turn last to the consideration of the consequences of belief for prayer, spirituality and vision of life.

Further Reading

Curran, Charles. *Themes in Fundamental Moral Theology* (Notre Dame: 1977).

Fairlie, Henry. *The Seven Deadly Sins Today* (Notre Dame: 1979).

Gustafson, James. *Protestant and Roman Catholic Ethics* (Chicago: 1978).

Menninger, Karl. *Whatever Happened to Sin?* (New York: 1973).

Oates, Wayne. *The Struggle To Be Free* (Philadelphia: 1983).

O'Brien, David (ed.). *Renewing the Earth: Catholic Documents on Peace, Justice and Liberation* (Garden City: 1977).

Sahakian, William. *Ethics: An Introduction to Theories and Problems* (New York: 1974).

U.S. Catholic Bishops. *The Challenge of Peace* (Pastoral on Nuclear War) (Washington: 1983).

12

All Our Secrets Are the Same

"O my soul, be prepared for the coming of the Stranger. Be prepared for him who knows how to ask questions."
T.S. Eliot (1888–1965)

"If we do not worship," as we have already quoted Peter Shaffer, "we shrink." Prayer has been conceived by most cultures, at least until the age of secularity, as a vital component of emotional maturity.

Prayer, Christianity holds, changes people. At a primary level, it reminds them who they truly are and what they are meant to be. It strengthens and sustains humanity by the assurance that they are not alone or forgotten, either in joy or in woe. Prayer is often said to "center" an individual, to allow the person to stop the ordinary busy-ness process to reflect on the how and why of all our activity.

Prayer itself shows many faces. It may be formulary, or a spontaneous cry of the heart. It may be intensely private, be shared with a friend, or take place within a situation of considerable ritual. Whether it be wordless or liturgical, mystical or petitionary, thanksgiving or adoration, prayer has as one of its central meanings the awareness of the individual of the ongoing presence of God in the heart of the person, and in the heart of the human experience. Prayer is not so much a turning from "the world" to some murky "other world" as it is a spirited awareness of the divine depths that God has intermingled with the depths of humanity.

To enter into prayer, then, is to enter into the depths. In a way, it is to pause and to remember: who we are, who God is; the ways in which our destinies are joined in the incarnation. That is Christianity's claim. Prayer means an openness to the God made manifest in Jesus, a God who is present to the core-mystery of each and all, a God who is present constantly, uniquely and intensely.

Christians of the twentieth century in the three great groupings of the faith—Roman Catholic, Orthodox and Protestant—have much more that unites them than divides them. In the area of prayer, historically, they have had differing emphases. Roman Catholic Christians, while having the Eucharist as their central worship experience, have accumulated a series of peripheral prayer formulas used in community. Though these are less in evidence in Catholicism today than previously, these would include such devotions as novenas, rosaries, litanies and benediction.

Protestants have had a two-pronged revisionary approach coming out of the Reformation. They have placed great stress on spontaneous or heartfelt prayer, with particular emphasis on the preached Word as a particularly intense religious experience. Part of the drive of Catholicism's Second Vatican Council was to recover much of that same centrality within itself. Additionally, Protestantism has taken Luther's lead of seeing work in the world, or vocation in the "secular" sense, as its own, highly valid form of prayer.

Orthodoxy, the remaining ancient and highly visible grouping of the Christian faith, directs much of its emphasis to a particularly solemn and mystical liturgical experience. To experience the full solemnity of Orthodox liturgy is to enter a world in which the divine things are so keenly evoked that the sense of divine presence can be very intense.

American life-styles in particular seem to work against a prayerful approach to living: both the need to take occasional time apart for quiet, and the ability to work with patience and calm assurance rather than franticness. Thomas Merton (1915–1968), one of America's most original Christian thinkers in the twentieth century, considered this subject often from his Kentucky Abbey of Gethsemani. In *Thomas Merton, Monk*, one of his friends, a psychologist and monk, David Steindl-Rast, noted Merton's reflections after a visit with him:

> In prayer we discover what we already have. You start where you are and you deepen what you already have, and you realize that you are already there. We already have everything, but we don't know it and we don't experience it. Everything has been given to us in Christ. All we need is to experience what we already possess.
>
> The trouble is, we aren't taking the time to do so. . . . If we really want prayer, we'll have to give it time. We must slow down to a human tempo and we'll begin to have time to listen.
>
> The best way to pray is: stop. Let prayer pray within you, whether you know it or not. This means a deep awareness of our true inner identity. It implies a life of faith, but also of doubt. You can't have faith without doubt. Give up the business of suppressing doubt. Doubt and faith are two sides of the same thing. Faith will grow out of doubt.

Christianity recognizes the fact of two great liturgies at work in the world: the sacred and the secular. The sacred liturgy is time apart to pray, converse with God, worship, reflect on the true self. Secular liturgy is a task in the world to carry on the work and demands of Jesus for dignity, wholeness, justice, peace and true happiness. Thus, one's career, faithfully and expertly carried out, is a kind of prayer of action; so is parenthood or friendship, or possibly political, social, business, arts or sports involvement. The secular and sacred liturgies mesh together: neither is sufficient unto itself; each helps to make sense of the other.

Of course the sacred liturgies of Christianity are diverse. All involve taking sacred time and sacred space apart to get in touch with the Source of our meaning, our hope and our significance. Liturgy represents a reaching in time to be touched by the timeless; it evokes the inexhaustible, loving, world of grace.

Some Christian traditions have very structured liturgies and are even dubbed "high church" as a result. The best known of these are Eastern Orthodox, Roman Catholic and Episcopal. Other traditions, such as Baptist and Methodist, have structured worship experience, but they are more free-form, with greatest emphasis on the preaching of the Word.

Within the high church traditions are to be found liturgical cycles, reflective of the great themes of Christianity. Thus, Advent and Christmas emphasize the incarnation in particular as Lent and Easter reflect on the resurrection. In most of the traditions, the Scriptures are read in a three-year cycle as part of the worship service.

In some ways, the "canons" or orders of service used in liturgies often reflect a summary statement of Christian belief and praxis (action). Consider these excerpts from the Fourth Eucharistic Prayer of Roman Catholic usage:

Father, you so loved the world
that in the fullness of time you sent your only Son to be our
Savior.
He was conceived through the power of the Holy Spirit,
and born of the Virgin Mary,
like us in all things but sin.
To the poor he proclaimed the good news of salvation,
to prisoners, freedom,
and to those in sorrow, joy.
In fulfillment of your will
he gave himself up to death;
but by rising from the dead
he destroyed death and restored life.

And that we might live no longer for ourselves but for him
he sent the Holy Spirit from you, Father,
as his first gift to those who believe,
to complete his work on earth
and bring us the fullness of grace. . . .
Remember those who take part in this offering,
those here present and all your people,
and all who seek you with a sincere heart.
Remember those who have died in the peace of Christ
and all the dead whose faith is known to you alone.
Father, in your mercy, grant also to us, your children,
to enter into our heavenly inheritance
in the company of the Virgin Mary, the Mother of God
and your apostles and saints.
Then, in your kingdom, freed from the corruption of sin and
death,
we shall sing your glory with every creature through Christ our
Lord,
through whom you give us everything that is good.

The excerpt, admittedly, was a long one. But consider the
themes of Christianity invoked in so short a compass: the loving
paternity and care of God, the incarnation, the social thrust and
personal call of Jesus' work, the need for personal and social
transformation, the power of the Holy Spirit, the resurrection
power that breaks down death and reaches for the Kingdom.

The Exultet, the ancient seventh century Christian hymn now
used at the Easter Vigil, stresses the theme of the resurrection in
a highly poetic way:

This is the night when Jesus Christ
broke the chains of death
and rose triumphant from the grave. . . .

Night truly blessed when heaven is wedded to earth
and humanity is reconciled with God.

May the Morning Star which never sets find this flame still
burning:
and shed his peaceful light on all mankind.

Similarly, the Preface of Christmas summarizes the incarnation:

In the wonder of the Incarnation,
your eternal Word has brought to the eyes of faith
a new and radiant vision of your glory.
In him we see our God made visible
and so are caught up in the love of the God we cannot see.

All three of these excerpts have come from the prayers for
the Eucharist. Considered a sacrament by most of the Christian
churches, the Eucharist is the celebration of the Lord's Last Supper, the Passover meal that Jesus had with his disciples on the evening of his betrayal. At the meal, as presented in John's account,
he opened his heart to his dearest friends. And as portrayed in the
Synoptic accounts, he passed bread and wine among them:

Now as they were eating, Jesus took some bread, and when
he had said the blessing he broke it and gave it to his disciples.
"Take it and eat," he said, "this is my body." Then he took
a cup, and when he had returned thanks he gave it to them.
"Drink all of you from this," he said, "for this is my blood,
the blood of the covenant which is to be poured out for many
for the forgiveness of sins" (Mt 26:26–28).

The account in 1 Corinthians 11 adds:

Whenever you drink it, do it as a memorial to me.

From these beginnings, Christianity has taken one of its most
profound acts of worship, and surrounded it with formulations and

solemnity. Many of the traditions, the high church in particular, speak in terms of a "real presence" of Christ physically in the consecrated bread and wine. In the Eucharist, in this understanding, some*thing* has become some*one*. Personalization is thus seen as the heart of liturgy, faith and the life process at-large. The believer receives in his or her own person the very reality of Jesus and of all that he stands for. For most Christian bodies, it is small wonder that the celebration of Eucharist or Lord's Supper—this joining of one's self to the Lord at the most intimate and intense point of his life and mission—is an awesome moment of worship.

Not only the Roman tradition, of course, but the others we have noted, Protestant and Orthodox, reserve some of their most striking formulations for the celebration of the Eucharist. The Orthodox liturgy of St. Basil:

> We presume to draw nigh unto thy holy altar, and presenting unto thee the figures of the holy body and blood of thy Christ, to call upon thee and beseech thee, O thou holy of holies, that thou wouldest be graciously pleased that thy Holy Spirit may come upon us and upon these gifts set forth, to bless, hallow, and declare this bread indeed the precious body of our Lord and God and Saviour Jesus Christ, and what is in this cup the precious blood of thy Christ.

John Calvin's Strassburg formulary of 1545 shows forth not only the earnestness, but the sometimes dire theological themes as well of that major sixteenth century reformer:

> In steadfast faith may we receive His body and blood, yea Christ Himself entire, who being true God and true man, is verily the holy bread of heaven which gives us life. So may we live no longer in ourselves, after our nature which is entirely corrupt and vicious, but may He live in us and lead us to that life that is holy, blessed and everlasting; whereby we

may truly become partakers of the new and eternal testament, the covenant of grace.

John Wesley, founder of Methodism in the eighteenth century, was fond both of extemporaneous and ritualized prayer. His Eucharistic service reads in part:

Ye that do truly and earnestly repent of your sins and are in love and charity with your neighbors and intend to lead a new life, following the commandments of God and walking from henceforth in his holy ways; Draw near with faith, and take this holy Sacrament to your comfort.

The power of the Eucharist also points to the significance of the sacraments at large in the Christian faith. They have been mentioned briefly before in this text as physical channels through which the grace of God is mediated. Practically all the churches accept baptism, the washing away of sinfulness and initiation into "the Way," and the Eucharist. The high church traditions speak of seven sacraments: in addition to baptism and Eucharist, they celebrate the sacraments of confirmation, reconciliation, anointing of the sick, ordination to ministry and marriage. Thus, at critical life points, God is seen as physically, palpably present to the individual: birth (baptism), growth (confirmation), nurture (Eucharist), forgiveness and new beginnings (reconciliation), decline and diminishment (anointing of the sick), community service (ordination), and love commitment (marriage).

The sacraments take very ordinary things—water, oil, bread, wine—and suggest that these, indeed all things material and human, are charged with possibilities by God. They indicate that the ordinary always bears the possibility of the extra-ordinary, that the sacred is never far from the secular.

Christianity does not claim that only in the sacraments are

forgiveness, nurture, commitment to be found. Quite the opposite. It maintains that the sacraments solemnize and celebrate for
the Christian community those realities with which God has
seeded the earth and its peoples. The sacraments do not invent or
create God's grace; they evoke the presence of God in all human
life and focus and intensify it.

Not surprisingly, Christian thinkers have used that same image of the focus in their description of Christ. God is said to be
like the sun that always shines and gives its good effects across
the earth without exception. But the sun's rays can be focused and
magnified in a magnifying glass and then they can gather to a
greatness, burst into flame, and become a fuller source of light,
warmth and hope. That focus, the image continues, is none other
than the figure of Jesus.

In addition to the formality of Eucharist, liturgy, preaching
and sacraments, much of Christianity has one other patterned approach to prayer: the Divine Office. Used primarily in monastic
situations, it also has enjoyed a revival among laity in this century.
Basically, the Office is a series of readings from the Book of
Psalms which are used in four-week cycles. The Psalms are one
of the most powerful expressions of Judaism and Christianity, en-
capsulating the whole range of human needs, emotions, hopes and
desperations. Not only do the Psalms reflect the human experience; they portray the closeness of God to all things human, as
well as the unending fidelity of God.

The most famous of all Christian prayers is termed "The
Lord's Prayer" and is a series of acknowledgments of God as both
parental and Other; as the source of all that we are and need; of
our own human failings and of our need to be restored and pro-
tected by the divinity. It also makes use of that organizing symbol
we have already noted in the message of Jesus: the kingdom. The
prayer asks most centrally that the kingdom or reign of God at last
will arrive so that all might at last be what it was meant to be:

Our Father in heaven,
may your name be held holy,
your kingdom come,
your will be done,
on earth as in heaven.
Give us today our daily bread.
And forgive us our debts
as we have forgiven those who are in debt to us.
And do not put us to the test,
but save us from the evil one (Mt 6:9–13).

The mention of the kingdom raises the final ultimate consideration of Christianity. Where does it all go: the world, our ideals and drives, our struggles, our failures and successes, our loves and our hates? This study of the last things is classically called eschatology from the Greek word *eschaton*, last things.

In listening closely to the questions of eschatology, we hear the often hidden cry of every human heart. We remember Thoreau's sobering phrase that most people lead lives of quiet desperation. For it is when we ask about our own most primal, intimate hopes, nightmare fears, fundamental longings, loves and lack of loves, that we also ask the most primal and universal questions. In this sense, all our secrets are the same. And we do well not to cheapen such profundities with facile answers or constant considerations.

Christianity is sober and sparing in its treatment of life beyond this life. "Eye has not seen, ear has not heard what God has prepared for those who love him" (1 Cor 2:9). "We see now through a glass darkly, but then face to face" (1 Cor 13:12). That which is to be will in some way be continuous with what has been, as the Risen Christ is continuous with the earthly Jesus. Humanity enters another dimension of being in which all that has been of worth, power, goodness, truth or beauty is taken up into the core reality of the human person and thus survives into communion with God. The images of the afterlife in both the Hebrew and

Christian Scriptures tend to portray joyous, community, physical occasions: banquets and weddings.

There is an element of judgment in this kingdom. God gives to each an invitation to fullness of life in some way. Each person makes a response in life or in death. And to the extent that the choice is full and free, God allows each individual the consequences of that choice. If one opts for utter isolation, and the total rejection and disdain of others, one in a sense has chosen what traditionally is known as hell, total distance from God. Significantly, at the pit of Dante's *Inferno,* one finds not fire but ice, symbolic of the betrayal and desertion of all that is human.

T.S. Eliot graphically shows the reality of judgment in Christian understanding in the *Choruses from the Rock.* The Stranger—Eliot's designation for God—is the one who above all knows how to ask of each individual the personal and most ultimate of all questions:

> O my soul be prepared for the coming of the Stranger.
> Be prepared for him who knows how to ask questions.

In summary, in Christian faith, it is ultimately the integral person in his or her most intimate core which survives. When the physical universe yields to entropy or disintegrates, the personal alone survives, having all that is vital and good transubstantiated into itself. These ultimate persons then live on with one another, and face to face with God. If the immensity of this seems all too vast, if the scenario seems all too unimaginable in the literal sense of the term, Christianity can point to the schemas of modern physics and astronomy and ask if they are really more graspable.

Precisely because these final things are so laden with mystery, Christian thought has been fascinated to find ways to reimage the reality so that the heart comes alive with its hope, even if the mind cannot picture it clearly. The most stunning medieval example of this style is the one we have often cited: Dante's *Di-*

vine Comedy. And in twentieth century English, C.S. Lewis's Narnian Chronicles, especially *The Lion, The Witch and The Wardrobe*, the first of a seven novel set, are amazingly effective in picturing Christian thought and its eschatological hopes in a story that children and adults alike find compelling. The inside of reality, Lewis concludes in *The Last Battle*, is larger and truer than the outside.

Sometimes it is not the theologians or philosophers who receive the most penetrating and evocative insights about the great and final realities; it may well be the musician or the artist. To listen either to the instrumental or choral Bach, to look steadily at a Rouault Christ-clown, is also to peer at ultimacy. It was composer Gustav Mahler (1860–1911) who wrote this poem to accompany his Resurrection Symphony (1895):

Believe, my heart, you have lost nothing.
Everything you longed for is yours; yes, yours.

You were not born in vain.

You have not lived and suffered in vain.
What has been must go.

What has gone will rise again.
Stop trembling.
Get ready to live.
O Pain, all-penetrating one,
I have escaped you.
O Death, all-conquering one,
Now you are conquered.
With wings I have won for myself,
In fervent love I shall soar

To the Light unseen.

I shall die to live.
You will rise again, my heart, in a moment.

With this look at Christian worship and eschatology, we conclude the searching of main-line Christianity for its reading of the ultimate things. It may not be altogether inappropriate to pose to Christianity-at-large the questions asked of other thinkers in earlier chapters about the nature of the universe, humanity, the flaw and the remedy.

The Universe. The Christian universe is one in which a God who is Ground and fullness of being, who is personal and compassionate, creates all that is from nothingness. In the beginning is God. Period. This God is energy and dynamism, is interpersonal and in love creates all that exists to share some measure of life.

Humanity. In the vast creative process of which God is Lord, humanity is privileged and called in a special way, individually and collectively, to share in God's creative capacities. As a gift from God, the creature shares in knowledge, will and profound emotion. Humanity is called upon to receive these gifts worthily and make them truly their own, taking on identities of their own, "true faces" with which to meet the Face of God.

Flaw. But humanity, given freedom by God, is quite capable of turning to its own agenda, of substituting lesser goods for ultimate Good. Humanity always lives with the threat and allure of idols, false urgencies and ultimacies. It turns, in fact, from the light and opts at times for darkness. The climate of this darkness is in part what Christianity means by "original sin." In this climate of sinfulness and diminishment, humanity finds itself in the "land of unlikeness," alienated from its true possibility.

Remedy. The Christ comes forth from God, true God and true human to break the alienation, to show who God truly is and how humanity might share in the very life of God, its true and overarching destiny. To enter into this Christ, either articulately and dramatically, or inarticulately (by standing for what the Christ stands for whether one has heard his name or not), is to enter a process that can lead to the fullness of life. Such fullness demands a slow process that includes risk, sacrifice, prayer, holiness, work, service, faith, hope, charity, virtue and transformation.

One of the most constant themes of western literature is the longing to go home. It runs our literary gamut from Odysseus and his crew in the *Odyssey* down to E.T. trying desperately to get a spaceship back to his home planet. It was St. Augustine who wrote one of the most famous lines in all Christian literature on the first page of his *Confessions:* "Thou hast made us for Thyself, O Lord, and our hearts are restless until they rest in Thee." He, too, was talking about going home, that place where one was truly loved and loving, where one was truly one's self.

In the surest sense, the search through the ultimate questions has also been an attempt to find a home, an identity, a true north on the chaotic compass of the modern. It is one thing to seek out a home, even to secure and to protect it; it is quite another to live in it worthily and make it one's own. That is the unending task of the ultimate questioner. T.S. Eliot wrote in *Little Gidding:*

> We shall not cease from exploration,
> And the end of all our exploring
> will be to arrive where we started
> and know the place for the first time.

To find the ordinary and extraordinary within one another; to discover that we carry around within us that which we are racing around so desperately to seek—these are some of the mysteries and allurements of the ultimate considerations. Dag Hammarskjold (1905–1961), the Swedish diplomat who became Secretary General of the United Nations, spent a life joining action and contemplation, search and discovery. We end these pages with his famous affirmation from *Markings:*

I don't know Who—or what—put the question. I don't know when it was put. I don't even remember answering. But at some moment I did say Yes to Someone, or Something. From that hour I was certain that existence is meaningful and that my life in self-surrender had a goal.

Further Reading

Feiner, Johannes and Vischer, Lukas (eds.). *The Common Catechism* (New York: 1975). An important breakthrough book in giving a common statement of faith for Catholics and Protestants. See especially the section on prayer, pp. 348–78.

Holmes, Urban. *A History of Christian Spirituality* (New York: 1981).

Leith, John. *Creeds of the Churches*. 3rd ed. (Atlanta: 1982).

Merton, Thomas. *New Seeds of Contemplation* (New York: 1961).

Schoonenberg, Peter. *God's World in the Making* (Techny: 1964).

Teilhard de Chardin, Pierre. *The Divine Milieu* (New York: 1960).

Thompson, Bard (ed.). *Liturgies of the Western Church* (Cleveland: 1962).